AMAZING GRACE

By Hal Lindsey

WESTERN FRONT, LTD, PUBLISHING COMPANY
PALOS VERDES, CALIFORNIA

ISBN 0-9641058-4-5

Western Front, Ltd.

Scriptures quoted in this book are from the New American Standard Bible (NASB) unless otherwise noted.

Book design/typography: Publication Services
Printing: Griffin Printing
Manufactured in the United States of America

TABLE OF CONTENTS

CHAPTER 1

HOW I MET "GRACE"

Amazing grace, how sweet the sound,
That saved a wretch like me!
I once was lost, but now am found,
Was blind, but now I see.

—CAPTAIN JOHN NEWTON

T he fog was so thick I could not see the bow of my boat on the Mississippi River. Despite the horrid conditions I knew I had to ferry several oil drilling crew members across the river. I worked in a tough area about sixty-five miles south of New Orleans.

At the age of twenty-five I was a devout pagan and a tugboat captain who worked hard and played even harder in the city of New Orleans.

Quickly, I tried to start up the generator that powered the radar. I tried once and it wouldn't start. I tried to prime it — nothing. Without radar in dense fog you have no idea what's happening on that old river.

Without a generator, I also didn't have compressed air to operate the signal horn. So I couldn't even give the danger signal if I heard a steamship bearing down on me.

With the constantly changing river currents and huge steamships barreling downriver on one of the busiest sea lanes in the world, the Mississippi was extremely dangerous even in good weather. But in this kind of weather — it was absolutely spooky.

Most captains would call a trip across the river under these conditions, without a radar or a signal horn, attempted suicide. At the very least a strong death wish was required. It was strange that none of the regular captains would show up for work when the fog got bad. And since I was a relief captain — well, you get the picture. I was always filling in at the most dangerous places under the most dangerous conditions.

"We're not going anywhere tonight," I announced after the third futile attempt to start the generator. "Even I don't feel like playing Russian roulette with steamships tonight."

"To hell with the fog," the head tool pusher retorted. "Just do your job and get us across the river. We have an emergency out at the drilling platform and we've got to get there."

"Okay, okay — it's your necks," I replied with a bit of false bravado. "But if we get lost out there in the middle of a bunch of steamships, don't come crying to me. Incidentally, if we get hit, you'll have about five seconds for your last words. If you're religious, you'd better pray now to avoid the rush."

So with only a compass and a stopwatch, we shoved off and blindly steered into the thick "pea soup" toward what I hoped would be the dock on the other side.

When we got to about the middle of the mile-and-a-quarter-wide river, my heart almost froze. I could hear the sound of the huge ship's engine coming straight toward us. I heard the steamship's horn blaring the danger signal as the river pilot picked us up on his radar. I couldn't even see the bow of my boat, much less the other ship.

HELP FROM AN UNSEEN HAND

I pulled the throttle back and hopelessly stared into the blackness. I realized that this was probably the time that I was going to cash in my chips. I thought, "God, I wish I could've found You." Then something utterly unexplainable happened. Something like an invisible force caused me to spin the helm (steering wheel) to the right. We immediately hit a glancing blow to the huge ship, just behind the bow. Then we rubbed up against it and slid along its side all the way to the stern and bounced off.

We were inches away from being hit broadside. We would have been smashed to pieces and pushed to the bottom of the river in seconds. There would have been no survivors.

I heard the tough drilling crew for the first time using God's name *not* in vain. These tough guys were scared stiff. "Skipper," they asked, "do we have a chance of making it to the other side?"

Once I slowed the boat down, we were totally lost in the fog. My prefigured compass heading and speed settings were now useless. By a miracle we dodged away from another ship and ran aground on the other side of the river — not too far from my dock. We then literally felt our way to the dock.

The drilling crew got off without their usual wise-cracks. They were almost "reverent." I laughed at them and taunted, "Come back and see me real soon. You're such brave guys — maybe we can make it back across the river before the fog lifts."

I wasn't really afraid while all the action was going on, but later that night I got a little shaken. I thought about what would happen if my life had suddenly ended that night. I wondered, "If there is a God, is He trying to tell me something?" It did seem to me that He was trying to get my attention. I also wondered what mysterious force caused me to turn at the last critical second.

My life began to flash before me like a video on fast-forward. Attempts to find some redeeming factor in those wasted years seemed almost ludicrous. I realized that if there was life after death, and if there was this place called Hell, I was well on my way there.

Then, like a bolt of lightning, I remembered the words of an elderly gentleman from a Mission off Times Square I had encountered almost five years earlier. Everything he had told me came racing back into my mind. The memory of his words so shook me that I determined to find out if Jesus Christ was for real or not.

QUESTIONS, QUESTIONS

My life's journey began in Houston, Texas. When people read my books, sometimes they imagine that I was raised on the pew of a church. But that was not the case. My folks weren't churchgoers. If my mother on rare occasions decided to attend, she would drag me along — usually over my objections.

I remember at age six we had one of those rare visits to a church. I tried to pay attention to the minister but was unable to understand him. And the way he shouted really made me wonder if he thought we were all hard of hearing. At that age, I thought God must be living on some distant planet and I would never have a chance to meet Him.

By the time I was a spunky ten-year-old, my curiosity seemed to grow as big as my home state. At home and school I never stopped asking questions. I wanted to know every-thing — from how they put lead in a pencil to how they dig tunnels underwater. But the biggest questions were those I asked myself at night when I would lie on my back outside

our little three-room shotgun house and stare up at the stars. I
would wonder, "Is there really a God out there? If there is,
does He know who I am — does He care?"

RELIGIOUS INOCULATION NO. 1

I remember the Sunday morning I decided to visit a
church and the pastor said, "If you want to become a
Christian, walk down to the front."

I was only twelve, but I was sincere about wanting to
know God. I walked forward and began to talk with a counselor. He said, "You are going to join the church, aren't
you?"

That's not why I came forward, but I replied, "Sure, if
that's what I am supposed to do."

Then he queried, "You do want to be baptized, don't
you?" "Yes, I guess so," I answered. But I was confused. I
had no idea what I had done. I had hoped they would explain
things to me.

Even though I joined the church and was baptized in
water, I still did not understand what it meant to be forgiven
by Christ.

As a result of what I learned in that church in the next
few months, I came to the conclusion that life was like a giant
balancing scale. If I did more good things than bad things,
the scale would tip in my favor and I'd make it to heaven.
But I already saw that the scale was tipping heavily in the
wrong direction.

My commitment didn't last. A dedication of the flesh
won't last very long. After a few months I realized I still had
more questions than answers. God didn't seem real. I
learned very little about Jesus, and He certainly wasn't real to
me either. I never even heard the word grace.

RELIGIOUS INOCULATION NO. 2

When I was fifteen I wondered, "Why is life so complicated?" Conflicts at home were erupting into volcanoes and my personal life was becoming a tangled net of emotions I didn't understand.

Even with the growing hostility, my heart somehow yearned for peace with God. I found another church and walked the aisle when the invitation was given. Like a vaccination, I was hoping it would "take" this time.

Again, I was told to join the church and be baptized. They advised me of all the "don'ts" I had to obey to be a Christian — "Don't smoke, drink, dance, fornicate, gamble or go to movies." As a serious athlete, I already didn't do most of the things on the "Christian taboo list." If only these people would have told me about salvation by grace through faith.

The net result was more dedication, more failure and more of a sense of guilt and alienation. I still had no understanding of what Jesus had done for me, much less how to know Him personally.

Socially, I was in a game of tug-of-war. My fellow athletes were bragging about their wild parties and their sexual exploits. So I often thought, "Am I missing out on life? God is no more real to me than He is to them. Is religion just cramping my style?"

Again, I began to drift away from church. The harder I tried to be good, the more I fouled up. Guilt drove me away and peer pressure finally prevailed. If everyone else was doing it, why not me? By the time I reached my seventeenth birthday, the battle that raged inside was tearing me apart. Every night a deep sense of shame was causing me to toss and turn. I thought, "If there is a God, He must be really steamed at a horrible person like me."

RELIGIOUS INOCULATION NO. 3

In my quest to find God, I went with a friend to yet another church. For the third time, I responded to the invitation, signed the membership card and was baptized.

Another false start. Everybody wanted me to join their church, but I just wanted to find Jesus — and nobody seemed to be able to tell me how to know Him.

From baseball I learned that "three strikes and you're out." And that's how I felt about God. I felt they were more interested in getting me into their church program than explaining how to know Jesus Christ.

If I couldn't really know the Lord, and religion was only cramping my style, what was the use? That was it! As far as I was concerned I would never darken the door of a church again. "Why have all the liabilities with none of the assets?" I thought.

I reasoned that I had done my part, but God didn't do His. As a bitter young man, I dove headlong into the pool of hedonism — and believe me, I was a good swimmer in that cesspool.

At the University of Houston I enrolled in "Partying 101," and for two years majored in booze and sex. Did my conscience bother me? Only at first. Before long even my sense of guilt turned numb.

ON DUTY IN TIMES SQUARE

I didn't want to think about the war that was escalating in Korea, but Uncle Sam had other ideas. My grades were more like a submarine than a supersonic jet, and I couldn't justify an academic deferment.

Who wanted to trudge in the mud with the North

Koreans? Not me. I rushed out to join the U.S. Coast Guard and was soon assigned to the U.S. Coast Guard Training School in New London, Connecticut.

The first two friends I met had connections in New York City — one guy's father was vice president of a huge corporation who had a permanent suite at a posh hotel near Central Park. That's where we stayed on several weekends. I thought, "It doesn't get much better than this — this is the life!"

One day, however, The Big Apple turned sour. I went to New York and the suite was not available. After drinking away our paychecks in a night of non-stop partying, a sailor friend and I spent Saturday morning on Times Square trying to bum enough to get something to eat. It didn't work. No one seemed interested in helping a couple of hungover sailors.

About the mid-afternoon I spotted a big sign just off Times Square that said, "Free Food!" When I looked closer, there was a smaller sign beneath it that said, "Jesus Saves." I laughed and said, "Hey, let's get those Holy Joes to feed us, they ought to be good for something!"

AN UNEXPECTED ENCOUNTER

When you're hungry, not even your contempt for Christianity stands in the way. Eating was easy. Exiting proved to be a bit more difficult. A well dressed man in his late fifties blocked the door and said, "Are you a Christian, young man?"

"I hope so," I replied without blinking — hoping that would get rid of him.

He didn't budge. The man said, "Sailor, I can tell by your answer that you are not a Christian."

I was in no mood to argue and said contemptuously, "You don't know me from Adam, so how can you know that? If I've learned anything from Christianity, it's that you can't be sure of anything." With great compassion, the mission worker said, "I understand how you feel. You see, if you were a Christian you would *know* it, not just hope so. But I don't think anyone has ever really told you why Jesus came to earth and what He is ready to give you."

I tried to brush off his remark, but he continued, "Sailor, it doesn't matter how bad or how good you've been. There is only one thing that matters — do you understand that when Jesus hung on that cross, God put every sin you would ever commit on Him. That judgment should have fallen on you, but He took the punishment of death in your place. And now He wants to give you His love and full pardon instead of His judgment. If you want to know the reality of God, all you need to do is accept the pardon Jesus purchased for you."

THE TRAGEDY OF "RELIGIOUS INOCULATION"

His words did not penetrate my hardened heart. By this time, I had been so inoculated with a caricature of Christianity that I couldn't recognize the genuine. I shoved him aside and laughed as my friend and I moved for the door. But I can still remember his final, cutting words. "Young man," he said, "you can reject me, but if you turn your back on God's gift of love and pardon, then His wrath will surely fall on you forever."

How ironic. His message was what I had searched for as a child, but by this time I was so hardened by false Christianity that I couldn't accept it.

But by God's grace, these very words came back to

me nearly five years later after nearly being killed on the Mississippi River.

A NOTE OF GRATITUDE

Parenthetically, years later, while going to Dallas Theological Seminary, I related this story to some fellow students who had gone to Princeton University. They asked me to describe the gentleman. They immediately identified him as the same wonderful man who worked at Princeton and discipled them. His name was Dr. Fullerton. I owe him for being the human link that brought me to the end of my quest to find God. He proved that God's Word doesn't return void.

BITTER WINE

The Coast Guard transferred me to the bawdy city of New Orleans, where I sank even deeper into a godless, anything-for-a-thrill lifestyle. Two and a half years later, when I received my military discharge, that's where I decided to stay. I had an apartment near the French Quarter that was already Action Central.

For the next couple of years I was a tugboat captain on the Mississippi River. My schedule was to work seven days on and seven days off. Every other week I climbed back on the tugboat exhausted and broke, nursing another humongous hangover. At the time I thought, "This is really living. New Orleans and I were made for each other."

As time passed, however, a strange phenomenon set in. The things that had always been such a thrill began to lose their excitement. I couldn't explain why, but the law of diminishing returns set in. I wondered, "What do I do for an

encore?" As the old saying puts it, the wine turned bitter, the women lost their luster and the songs mocked me.

The first quarter-century of my life can be summed up as a search to fill a growing sense of emptiness which nothing physical or sensual seem to fulfill.

I began to search for something — anything — that might explain why the things I thought would make me happy didn't anymore. I had become sick of my shallow playboy philosophy.

More and more, as I questioned people about their ideas on the problem, the conversation somehow led to whether there was a God or not.

Most of the people I ran with said, "Who cares?" Those who had a view usually felt their church's teachings were surely correct. But they usually felt that was a question to settle when you get "old."

And the Christian denominations were hopelessly at odds with each other, all claiming their way was the right way. Some went so far as to say theirs was the *only* right way. I reasoned, "They can't all be right! Are they all just as confused as I am?"

MY RABBIT'S FOOT

One sleepless night, everything came crashing in. My mind was tormented with questions and doubts that hovered over me like an immense dark cloud. I desperately needed some answers.

I thought maybe I should look at the Bible for myself. I reached to the bottom of my seabag and pulled out an old Gideons New Testament that I had never read. It had been given to me by faithful lady named Ms. Cravy when I was about twelve years old. I always carried it because I thought it was sort of a rabbit's foot to bring good luck.

I opened the pages to the beginning of the New Testament and started reading about the life of Jesus. Immediately, I became absorbed by the story. I thought, "I've heard what everyone else thinks about Jesus, but what does He say about Himself?"

When I reached the fifth chapter of Matthew, I got discouraged. The Sermon on the Mount teachings were way out of my league. When I read that looking after a woman to lust was the same in God's sight as committing adultery, I thought, "What man has a chance?" The only men I knew who didn't do that had another big problem — they liked other men.

"It's hopeless!" I concluded. "I've done a lot more than lust. There's no chance for someone like me." As I continued to read Christ's interpretation of the Ten Commandments I knew I could never, ever measure up.

I was about to close the book forever when I flipped over to another part of the New Testament. My eyes began to skim the pages of the Gospel of John, chapter three.

Jesus was having a conversation with a man who was filled with questions. His name was Nicodemus. I thought, "This fellow seems to be similar to me."

Christ told him, **"Except a man be born again, he cannot see the Kingdom of God"** (John 3:3 KJV).

"What in the world does being 'born again' mean?" I asked myself. Didn't the fact that I joined three churches and had been triple-dipped account for something?

It was then that God's Holy Spirit began to work on me. My life had been a never-ending struggle to escape from emotional stress and a horrible self-image. Even in high school, I had tons of ability, but was so torn inside that I was a failure at almost everything I started.

That night I thought, "Oh, I wish I could be born again and start from scratch with a clean slate." But what Jesus was talking about seemed impossible for a sinner like me.

I was so intrigued by the third chapter of John that I read it again and again and again. Suddenly it hit me that I could really be born again by simply believing that what Jesus did on the cross was for Hal Lindsey.

At that moment I had an overwhelming urge to pray, but didn't really know how. I looked up and said, "God if You are real, then show me how to believe." My faith didn't have a pulse and I wasn't even sure there was a God.

In the back of that Gideons Bible (the one that had been given to me during junior high school days) were instructions on how to become a Christian. It quoted the words of Jesus from Revelation 3:20, **"Behold I stand at the door and knock; if any one hears My voice and opens the door, I will come in to him, and will dine with him and he with Me."**

The instructions explained that the "door" is our will. We can choose to ask Christ into our lives and receive the forgiveness for our sins that was made available by His death.

Right there I said, "God, if this is true, I want Jesus Christ to come into my life and forgive me. If He can do that, then I accept Him right now." I pleaded with God to show me the truth.

When I woke up the next morning I was surprised to find myself reaching for the Bible. For the first time, the scriptures began to have meaning.

Two days later I was ready to begin my week of non-stop

partying. This time, however, things were different. The highs didn't seem so high. And those scriptures were flashing in my mind like neon signs.

A CRAZY PREACHER

The next week, when I returned to my riverboat, a deckhand came up to me and said, "Skipper, we've got a new boat-driver that's docked here and he's absolutely nuts. Every day he's down at the barroom preaching about Jesus."

The deckhand looked at me in disbelief when I said, "That's great. Tell him to come aboard. I'd like to ask him some questions about the Bible."

The next day, when the preacher-man came over, he was a little uncomfortable. After all, I had earned quite a reputation as a guy who liked to play jokes on people.

I tried to put him at ease by saying, "Last week something happened to me that I'd like to have your opinion about. They tell me you're a preacher."

"Yes, I'm a part-time pastor," he said as he began to ramble about his wife and six kids back in Alabama. "I've been out of work and this is the only place I could get a job." He wondered what he was doing in this God-forsaken city.

As I began to tell the preacher my story — how I had read the Bible and prayed — the man's mouth opened wider and wider. He looked like he was in a dentist's chair.

"So you're the reason," he began.

"What do you mean?" I asked.

"Don't you see it?" he exclaimed. "The Lord planned it so we would meet. Right here. Right now."

This jack-of-all-trades Assemblies of God lay preacher opened his well-worn Bible and read scripture after scripture to assure me that I had done the right thing.

When he finished, we prayed and I knew beyond any doubt that Christ had forgiven my sin and that I was truly born again.

Two days later, after telling me the vital importance of daily Bible reading, the man left. I never saw him again.

Even though I didn't start attending church (I didn't know where to go), changes began to happen in my life. Instead of heading for a drink, I found myself heading for my cabin to read God's Word. I didn't talk about it much, but the change in my lifestyle was so obvious to the crew that they became worried about me, as did the rest of my friends.

I remember the day one of my girfriends brought over a priest who basically said, "Don't get too worked up about the Bible — it will only confuse you. Just relax, attend the Mother Church and everything will be all right." In other words, leave the Bible to us professionals. You just come, pray, pay and stay. Somehow, I didn't buy that counsel.

GOING BACK TO HOUSTON

Six months had passed and I realized that if I was to grow as a Christian, I needed to get away from the hedonistic influence of the New Orleans scene. I headed for Houston, my hometown. I thought, "I hope I can find someone to help explain what the Bible really says."

It took the Lord nearly a year to get me "spiritually housebroken" enough to go to a church. I attended a little Baptist church for a while and received a lot of help from a pastor named Jack Blackwell.

While working at a series of short-term jobs, I usually spent my lunchtimes alone, reading the Bible. One day a fellow worker noticed what I was reading and said, "Our minister is going speak in a class at Rice University about the conflict in the Middle East. He's going to explain how it was predicted in the Bible. Would you like to come?"

I was intrigued, so I went along. I had never heard anything like it. For more than two and a half hours I listened in amazement at how the prophecies of the Bible were coming to pass.

That night I couldn't sleep. I checked out everything he said about fulfilled prophecy and became totally convinced that the Bible truly was the inspired Word of God.

I began attending his church and soon found myself studying scripture almost six to eight hours every day — plus holding a full-time job. My parents enjoyed having me back home, but were worried that I was being consumed by "religion."

"What has happened to you?" my Dad finally asked. He recalled visiting me about a year earlier in New Orleans, and how I had taken him on a shocking tour of the French Quarter. "Now you're here with a Bible under your arm — a totally different person. Can you help me understand the change?"

As I told my father what had happened, his eyes became moist and he said, "Hal, I wish I could know Jesus like you do."

That night, in the living room of our family home, we got on our knees and my father asked Jesus to come into his heart and be his Savior.

My mother didn't know what to think. She was a believer, but struggled with her daily Christian life. It wasn't long, however, until Jesus became very personal and real to her.

For the next two years, I became involved in intensive Bible study and attended church every time the doors opened.

THE BURNING BUSH

One day, as I was studying the book of Exodus, God showed me His plan for my life. It happened while I was reading the account of Moses at the burning bush. God clearly spoke to me and said, "You are going to be another bush through which I'm going to speak."

That came as quite a shock, since I was terrified of speaking in public. I had even quit speech class at the university because of my fear to speak in front groups.

I said, "Lord, if you want me to preach, it's going to take a miracle." The Lord reminded me of the conversation He had with Moses when He asked him to go before Pharaoh and say, **"Let My people go."** Moses responded, **"Please, Lord, I have never been eloquent, neither recently nor in time past, nor since You have spoken to Your servant; for I am slow of speech and slow of tongue"** (Exodus 4:10).

Here's what the Lord said to Moses. **"Who has made man's mouth? Or who makes him dumb or deaf, or seeing or blind? Is it not I, the Lord? Now then go, and I...will be with your mouth and teach you what you are to say"** (vv.11,12).

When I read those words and realized how God used Moses, I said, "Lord, I'm Yours. You made me, you have called me, and You put the right words in my mouth."

Before long I was asked to be the substitute teacher for an adult Bible class in Sunday School. I came to the room totally prepared, but my knees were knocking, my palms were sweating and my hands shook like I had palsy. "Okay, Lord,"

I prayed, "Remember how You helped Moses."

What an experience! As long as I kept my mind on the Word, I had confidence. But when I thought about my speaking, I nearly fainted.

Immediately after the class a woman asked if she could speak with me. "Young man," she said, "I believe God has singled you out to teach His Word far and wide someday, but your grammar is really offensive. Nobody is going to want to listen to you."

That didn't come as any surprise to me. But what she said next did. "I'm an English teacher," she said. "If you'll come twice a week to my home, I'll teach you proper grammar."

I accepted the offer, and within one year she brought me from third grade grammar to college level.

A COLLEGE DROPOUT IN SEMINARY?

At the same time my knowledge of Scripture was rapidly multiplying and the call of God was becoming stronger every day. I prayed, "Lord, if it is possible, I would like to study at a seminary."

On the surface, it was impossible. I was a college dropout and had no religious credentials. The school I set my sights on was Dallas Theological Seminary — one of the most distinguished evangelical graduate schools in the nation.

The Lord directed my attention to Psalm 71. All of a sudden God began to speak directly to me from this Psalm, **"O God, You have taught me from my youth; and I still declare Your wondrous deeds. And even when I am old and gray, O God do not forsake me, until I declare Your strength to this generation. Your power to all who are to come, For Your righteousness, O God, reaches to the**

**heavens, You who have done great things; O God, who is
like You? You, who have shown me many troubles and
distresses, will revive me again, and will bring me up
again from the depths of the earth"** (Psalm 71:17-20).

(God revealed to me in a very extraordinary experience with Him that these verses were both a promise and a
prophecy of His plan for me. Much of this prophecy has
already come true in my life. The promise in these scriptures
has seen me through some very dark hours during periods of
great personal trial. Now that my hair is turning "gray," it's
going to be interesting to see how the rest is fulfilled.)

CRACKING THE FAITH BARRIER

I was strengthened to believe God by this experience.
I reasoned, "If God could call me to speak on His behalf,
couldn't He also open the doors of a seminary?" As I mailed
my application to Dallas I took a deep breath. "They've never
seen anything this weak," I thought. I could almost hear them
laughing.

What I did not know was that my pastor, Bob
Thieme, had made a special visit to the seminary and spoken
with the admissions director. "Don't base your decision on
what you see on paper," he told them. "This young man is
serious. He taught himself basic Greek without anybody's
help. And he has a call from the Lord that burns in his heart."

The seminary sent me an IQ test to see if I could at
least do the work. The Lord gave me the ability to go through
it in such a way that I knew it would be a higher score than
any I had taken before.

Within two weeks I received a letter that read:
"Congratulations. You have been accepted as a student at
Dallas Theological Seminary."

"Hallelujah!" I shouted. "The miracle has happened!"

There was only one major problem. The recession of 1958 had left me without work and I was totally broke.

My parents wanted to help, but my mother said, "Hal, you've got to write the seminary and tell them you can't come. There must be others on a waiting list. Right now it's just impossible for your dad and me to spare the funds."

"Don't worry, Mom," I told her as I gave her a hug. "The Lord has opened the seminary door and *somehow* He's going to provide."

I walked into my bedroom, closed the door, and fell on my face before God. "Okay, Lord. It's all in Your hands."

A few minutes later, my mother came running into my room with the mail. "Here are several letters for you." (This was not a normal occurance.)

I couldn't believe it! Every envelope I opened contained a check. Nobody knew my financial problem, but the letters all had similar messages: "The Lord has impressed on us that we should help you with your seminary education. We will be praying for you."

It happened again and again, day after day. By the time I moved to Dallas there was enough money to pay my tuition and expenses for the whole semester. And that's the way it continued until the day I graduated.

SOMETHING EXTRAORDINARY
OUT OF THE ORDINARY

I've been in the Lord's work for more than 39 years now, and by the grace of God, I've seen many miracles worked in and through me. Perhaps the greatest has been the miracle of turning me into a best-selling author. Me, a guy who has always hated to write!

Now if the Lord, by His amazing grace, could untangle the threads of my messed-up life and use me to write books that have touched the lives of millions of people around the world, I know He can do wonders for you too.

Just as God turned Simon, the impetuous vacillator, into Peter, the Rock; and Saul, the ultimate legalist, into Paul, the champion of grace; so He delights in taking ordinary people and creating something extraordinary out of them. And this is usually in areas that are very different from what we were before being born again.

THE MIRACLE OF CAPTAIN NEWTON

At the age of eleven, in A.D. 1736, John Newton boarded a ship in London for a life at sea. He became a crusty, unfeeling captain of a slave ship. Then he met the grace of God and was so transformed that he denounced slavery and became an ordained minister.

As a new creation, Newton wrote his personal testimony in the form of a song: *"Amazing grace, how sweet the sound, that saved a wretch like me."* This hymn has become an all-time favorite of the whole Church.

These words in large measure tell my story, too: *"T'was grace that taught my heart to fear, and grace my fears relieved. How precious did that grace appear, the hour I first believed...."*

UNFINISHED PRODUCTS

I surely do not want to leave the impression that I think I'm a finished product. All Christians in this life are "unfinished products" in the hands of a gracious God. The process of pruning and cultivating continues day by day, season by season until we go home to Him.

BEWARE OF GALATIANISM

One of the greatest dangers I have both observed and been victimized by is the "tradition of the self appointed elders" in the Church. These men teach that there is grace before we are saved, but that we must live the Christian life by a strange mixture of the law principle with grace. This was the curse introduced to the Galatian churches.

God knows that as believers we are still very fallen beings. His grace is even more abundant after we are His beloved children. Paul brings this out clearly, **"Therefore, since we have been justified through faith, we have peace with God through our Lord Jesus Christ, through whom we *have gained access by faith into this grace in which we now stand.* And we rejoice in the hope of the glory of God"** (Romans 5:1-2 NIV).

I'm sad to say that some of the worst sins I have committed have been after salvation. But God's grace taught me to believe His promises of forgiveness and to get up and trust Him again.

Grace properly understood doesn't return void, nor does it promote loose living. But it does keep us from Satan's "guilt trap" in which we not only sin, but put ourselves on the shelf through unbelief in God's promises of forgiveness and restoration.

David testified concerning the secret of his life with God, **"If you, O Lord, kept a record of sins, O Lord, who could stand? But with you there is forgiveness; therefore**

you are feared [reverently trusted]. **I wait for the Lord, my soul waits, and in his word I put my hope"** (Psalm 130:3-5 NIV).

If God kept a record of our sins and held them against us, no one could stand. But there is forgiveness with Him for the purpose that we can trust Him and His Word. If you think God is holding past sins against you, you simply cannot believe Him now. The false guilt, fed by "the Accuser of the brethren," produces estrangement that will not let you believe His promises.

The reason God is able to deal with us in such amazing grace is the entire subject of this book. It was all provided for at great cost at the CROSS.

Are you still bound by forces that seem larger than life itself? I know how you feel. In my desperate search as a young believer, I had no idea what it meant to be redeemed, justified, reconciled, and forgiven. But I began to get free from the fears and guilt that kept me alienated from God, myself, and society when I learned about the manifold facets of what Christ did for me on the cross.

This book is about these things. May this book be a spiritual adventure for you that will lead you into the manifold splendor of the cross, and the grace it set into operation.

"For of His fulness we have all received, and grace upon grace" (John 1:16)

CHAPTER 2

WHAT IN THE WORLD IS WRONG WITH MAN?

Any medical doctor worth his salt knows he can't bring about a cure for a disease unless he first diagnoses the problem correctly. Politicians and statesmen must carefully and accurately assess the underlying causes of problems in their town or state or country before they can pass effective legislation to correct matters.

The same is true when seeking to understand the most perplexing and challenging question of all time: "Why does man think and behave as he does?"

There's no shortage of diagnoses for why we do the things we do. Whole fields of scientific study are devoted to this question. Psychology tries to find out why *individuals* think and act the way they do. Sociology specializes in the dynamics of *group* behavior.

But whether you've got one man alone or a whole group together, almost all rational thinkers today are trying to come to grips with what's wrong with human behavior, what's wrong with our institutions and what's wrong with the world.

MAN SEEN AS A QUIRK OF EVOLUTION

One suggested answer to this problem was set forth by Arthur Koestler in a talk given at the fourteenth Nobel Symposium in Stockholm in 1969. He said, "There have

been many diagnostic attempts made to explain man's abnor-
mal behavior, from the Hebrew prophets to contemporary
ethologists [scientists who study animal behavior]. But none
of them started with the premise that man is an aberrant
[abnormal] species, suffering from a *biological* malfunction."

He asked the question, "Is our aggressiveness towards
our fellowmen socially acquired, or is it biologically built in,
part of our genetic makeup and evolutionary heritage?"

Koestler pointed out that from the dawn of consciousness until the middle of the twentieth century, man had to live
with the prospect of his death as an *individual*. But since the
incredible forces of atomic power were unlocked three
decades ago, man now has to live with the prospect of his
death as a *species*.

Faced with this threat of self-extinction, one would
have expected man's aggressiveness to have become tempered
by reason.

"But," Koestler wrote, "appeals to reasonableness
have always fallen on deaf ears, for the simple reason that
man is not a reasonable being; nor are there any indications
that he is in the process of becoming one.

"On the contrary, the evidence seems to indicate that
at some point during the last explosive stages of the evolution
of Homo sapiens, something has gone wrong. There is a flaw,
some subtle engineering mistake built into our native equipment which would account for the paranoid streak running
through our history."[1]

While one may not agree with all of Arthur Koestler's
conclusions, the fact remains that he, too, has sought to give
an explanation of man's deviant behavior and has concluded
that we are stuck with a genetic quirk of nature for which
there is no hope of remedy.

ARE WE READY TO GO
"BEYOND FREEDOM AND DIGNITY"?

B. F. Skinner, the author of the controversial book *Beyond Freedom and Dignity* and the man who is thought by many to be the most influential living American psychologist, has his theories about the nature of man and how he functions best, yet they are diametrically opposed to Arthur Koestler's. Koestler felt man's *internal* mechanism was defective and the cause of his malfunction, while Skinner feels the entire problem of man's errant behavior lies in the *external* influences that affect him daily.

Skinner's solution to self-centered behavior is to place sufficient control over a man's external conduct and culture until he no longer has any inner freedom or free will. In this tightly controlled environmental state, men will refrain from polluting, overpopulating, rioting, making war, being selfish, greedy, unloving and arrogant — *not* because of the disastrous results of these actions, but because he has been conditioned to want what serves the group interests.

This may sound a little like the supposed utopia of George Orwell's *1984*, but this thinking is no joke to Dr. Skinner. Because of his many experiments with the controlled behavior of animals (and to a lesser degree with humans) many reputable thinkers have bought all or parts of this philosophy of behavioral control.

Although Skinner is strongly opposed by most humanists, religionists, and Freudian psychoanalysts, he steadfastly maintains that behavior is determined completely from without, *not* from within. He insists that any idea of a soul or inner man is a superstition that originated, like belief in God, from man's inability to understand his world and his own actions.

TWO OPPOSING CAMPS

If we were to follow B. F. Skinner's philosophy to its inevitable conclusions, we would be forced to admit that no man is responsible for his failure to behave correctly. He could simply plead that he was never "conditioned" to do the right thing. This would perhaps result in removing all sense of personal guilt from man, but it would also create civil and moral anarchy.

What we're really dealing with here in these two men's representative positions are two completely opposing views of man and of why he behaves the way he does. They both agree that man has a behavioral problem, but one view says it's an inner problem and the other says it's external. Nevertheless, in both camps *no* appreciable solution to the dilemma of how to start man behaving in an unselfish, loving, peaceful, generous, kind, patient and concerned manner has been discovered.

WHATEVER HAPPENED TO "SIN"?

For years most psychiatrists and psychologists have dismissed the old-fashioned religious idea of "sin" as irrelevant at best and downright dangerous at its worst. They've accused religion of producing guilt in its followers and have counseled patients to cast off their guilt feelings and do what they want.

But in the late '60s, one member of psychiatry's sacred inner circle defected from his previously held views of why man behaves improperly. Dr. Karl Menninger, world-renowned psychiatrist, says in his new book *Whatever Became of Sin?* that mental health and moral health are identical. He also said that the only way our suffering, struggling, anxious society can hope to prevent mental ills is by recognizing *the reality of sin.*

"If the concept of personal responsibility and answerability for ourselves and for others were to return to common acceptance," he says, "and man once again would feel guilt for sins and repent and establish a conscience that would act as a deterrent for further sin, then hope would return to the world."

Tragically, Menninger says he was prompted to write his new book after speaking to a group of young liberal theologians. They told him of their frustration and sense of inadequacy in trying to deal with the problems of their parishioners, and how they couldn't compete with the evil forces attracting their young people.

"It came to me," Menninger said, "that our clergymen have become shaken reeds, smoking lamps, earthen vessels...spent arrows."

His solution is to stand up and tell the world what its problem is. "Preach it! Tell it like it is. Say it from the pulpits. Cry it from the housetops!" says Dr. Menninger, psychiatrist, *not* evangelist!

A VIABLE ALTERNATIVE

Dr. Karl Menninger has not traded in his psychiatrist's couch for a pulpit, and certainly many people will find things in Menninger's views that they can't go along with completely, But he has done something many ministers have failed to do in our times. He's offered a diagnosis for man's problem which is the same one the Bible has taught. Man is a sinner and needs reconciliation with God, with his fellowman, and with himself.

SIN HAS CAUSED A BARRIER
BETWEEN GOD AND MAN

I would like to assume that anyone reading this book has come with an open mind and wants to understand the Bible's diagnosis of the human dilemma.

From the first book of the Old Testament to the last book of the New Testament, there is one consistent theme, and that is that God and man experience an alienation — a barrier, if you please — that man cannot remove and God says He already has.

Every error ever taught regarding man's relationship to God has historically begun with an improper understanding of sin and its devastating effect on man. There's no use talking about who Jesus was or why He came until we first understand the nature of the barrier that exists between man and his God.

If a couple came to me who were alienated from each other and had erected an insurmountable barrier between them, I could begin to help them resolve their conflict only when I got them to see how the barrier between them had come about.

THE UNIVERSAL BARRIER—
ITS CAUSES AND RESULTS

Picture if you will the first record we have of man's relationship with God. It was in a beautiful environment, and there was true fellowship and communication between God and man. Man was free to do as he wanted in all areas. He was asked to do only one thing — not to eat of a certain tree in the Garden. This was a test of man's trust in God's judgment and care for him.

It was also a test of whether he wanted to continue in the relationship. The tree itself was not evil; it was the choice to disobey God that was evil. That disobedient choice would give him an experiential knowledge of good and evil.

Now, that doesn't seem like much for God to ask. I used to ask my teenaged daughters not to do certain things. I knew that whether they obeyed me or not, to a certain degree, represented their love and trust of me. I could not force the obedience of a nineteen-year-old daughter, but I did expect her obedience as a recognition of respect for my judgment and care for her. I expected her to remember that over the years I had proven that I only had her best interest at heart.

Before Eve and then Adam decided to take a bite of that forbidden fruit, they had to believe a lie about God's character. They had to believe that God did not have their best interest at heart — that indeed He was keeping something from them that would make them god-like. The moment they disobeyed, an impossible barrier was raised between themselves and God. The wonderful relationship they had enjoyed with their Creator was instantly broken. At the very core of their being, spiritual life died. They no longer had the kind of life that God has.

That story is recorded in the first book of the Bible, the Book of Genesis; in the other thirty-eight books of the Old Testament and the twenty-seven books of the New, we have the continuing story of what God has done to reconcile man back to Himself. The Bible reveals a number of barriers so great that only God can remove them.

THE FOURFOLD BARRIER

Mankind erected four great barriers that hopelessly separate us from God. This wall of barriers is so impenetrable that all the religions, philosophies, idealisms, good works, and ingenuity of men can't tear it down.

The compelling reason that made me write this book is to pass on the best news I have ever heard — God Himself *has* torn down the barriers.

Let's look at the barriers first. Then we can fully appreciate what it cost God to abolish them!

---

1. *Los Angeles Times*, June 7,1970.

CHAPTER THREE

BARRIER NUMBER ONE:

GOD'S
HOLY
CHARACTER

Some of us know someone whose life is so pure and exemplary, who has such a goodness about him, that we're just a little uncomfortable in his presence. Especially if we have any idea that he knows about some of *our* grosser habits. We don't feel that way around most of our friends, though, because we know *they* live just like we do.

What do you suppose it is that makes us feel such a difference, almost an invisible barrier between the pure person and ourselves?

It is, of course, his saintly character.

We know we don't measure up to his standard of conduct, and we feel he might be inclined to be judgmental of us. So we feel an alienation of sorts.

To a much greater degree, that's the problem between God and man. The character of God is so flawless and the nature of man is so full of flaws that the very holiness of God becomes a barrier to man.

Now, before you say to yourself, "Well, it's God's fault, then, that man is alienated from Him. God needs to lower His standards if He wants to reconcile with man," we need to take a look at what the character of God is really like.

We're talking about a standard of character that's way

out of our league. Most of us can pick out ten people we know and measure ourselves up against their lives and not come off too badly. There's only one small problem when it comes to measuring ourselves against the character of God— it's perfect. There's no grading on the curve with God! If we want to be accepted by Him and brought back into reconciliation with Him, we must become as perfect as He is.

Impossible, you say?

Not so!

The story of how God went about making man acceptable again, after he lost his fellowship with God in the Garden of Eden, is the story we tell in this book. The first thing we must thoroughly understand is...

THE CHARACTER OF GOD

These are the component parts of the character of God as He has revealed Himself in His Word and His history of dealing with men. God's essence or character is made up of ten absolute attributes.

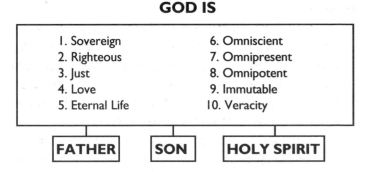

GOD IS

1. Sovereign	6. Omniscient
2. Righteous	7. Omnipresent
3. Just	8. Omnipotent
4. Love	9. Immutable
5. Eternal Life	10. Veracity

FATHER   **SON**   **HOLY SPIRIT**

All these attributes are found in the Father, Son, and Holy Spirit.

FIRST: GOD IS *SOVEREIGN*

God has a will. By Himself and with assistance from no one He makes decisions and policies and sets up principles. He has the right to do whatever He pleases.

The sovereignty of the Almighty was established even before creation. **"Even from eternity I am He; and there is none who can deliver out of My hand; I act and who can reverse it?"** (Isaiah 43:13). This attribute means that God has the right to do as He chooses.

God alone has written the "Policies and Procedures" manual for mankind. As the Psalmist wrote, **"Whatever the Lord pleases He does, in heaven and in earth"** (Psalm 135:6). **"Therefore know this day, and consider it in your heart, that the Lord Himself is God in heaven above and on the earth beneath; there is no other"** (Deuteronomy 4:39 NKJV).

His sovereignty is total. It extends to all of creation. **"The Lord reigns, He is clothed with majesty; The Lord is clothed, He has girded Himself with strength. Surely the world is established, so that it cannot be moved"** (Psalm 93:1 NKJV).

God always acts in accordance with all the other attributes of His character. So even though God has the right to do as He pleases, He can never act unfairly or untruthfully. This would contradict His attributes of justice and veracity. God *cannot* act contradictory to his own nature. He *cannot* express one attribute at the expense of another.

For example, a mother may tell a child he will receive a spanking if he plays with matches. But then, when the child plays with the matches and burns himself, she may forgo the spanking and, instead, hold him in her lap and love him. In that case she has expressed her love at the expense of her justice. She contradicted her word.

Not so with God. He finds a way to express His love, but never by compromising His justice.

Our security with God rests in the absolute realiability of God acting consistantly with His character. Since He is just, He will never choose to act unfairly. Since He is Love, He will always choose to act in our best interest.

God's sovereignty and love are seen working together for us in this promise, **"And we know that God causes all things to work together for good to those who love God, to those who are called according to His purpose"** (Romans 8:28).

GOD'S CALCULATED "RISK"

One very important factor of this attribute is that God made a sovereign choice to create mankind with will, intellect, emotion and moral reason that corresponds to His own personality. One of the reasons He did this was so that He could give us the ability to choose independently of His will. This was a calculated risk God was willing to take in order that He could create us with the ability to experience His love and to love Him back.

Without freedoom of choice, there can be no love nor fellowship. Robots cannot love. How our freedom to choose and God's sovereignty relate to each other is another great mystery, but we will tackle some of the implications as the book progresses.

(See also Deuteronomy 4:39;1 Chronicles 29:12; Psalm 47:2; 83:18; 93:1; 135:6; Daniel 4:35; Acts 17:24.)

SECOND: GOD IS *RIGHTEOUS*

God is absolute virtue and perfection. He is the standard of all that is right. He is morally perfect without a shadow of deviousness. For Him to do anything that is unfair, unjust or wrong is totally impossible. Just the opposite: God is the standard by which all righteousness is measured. **"Righteous are You, O Lord, And upright are Your judgments"** (Psalm 119:137).

God's Law, which He gave through Moses, is simply a tangible expression of His attribute of righteousness in terms that we can understand. As such, His commandments are as pure and blameless as He is. This is why David, the inspired Psalmist, wrote: **"The law of the Lord is perfect, converting the soul; The testimony of the Lord is sure, making wise the simple; The statutes of the Lord are right, rejoicing the heart; The commandment of the Lord is pure, enlightening the eyes; The fear of the Lord is clean, enduring forever; The judgments of the Lord are true and righteous altogether"** (Psalm 19:7-9).

David saw the glory of God's character in the law even though he knew he could not keep it perfectly.

(See also Ezra 9:15; Psalm 48:10; 145:17; Jeremiah 23:6; 1 John 2:29.)

THIRD: GOD IS *JUST*

God is absolutely just. It's impossible for Him to do anything that's unfair either to Himself or to man. He executes perfect justice in accordance with His attribute of righteousness. All that is unrighteous must be judged and separated from a relationship with God.

Moses said, **"He is the Rock, His work is perfect; for all His ways are justice, a God of truth and without injustice; righteous and upright is He"** (Deuteronomy 32:4 NKJV).

King David clearly saw this when he wrote, **"And do not enter into judgment with Thy servant. For in Thy sight no man living is righteous"** (Psalm 143:2). Isaiah also saw this truth: **"But we are all like an unclean thing, and all our righteousnesses are like filthy rags..."** (Isaiah 64:6 NKJV). Even our most sincere efforts at doing good works are totally unacceptable in the presence of God's righteousness and justice. These two attributes combined equal what we call God's holiness.

(See also Romans 1:18; Isaiah 45:21.)

FOURTH: GOD IS *LOVE*

God is perfect, infinite love. It's given freely and without any consideration to the loveliness or merit of the object. It includes His enemies as well as His friends.

What the world calls love is a billion-dollar industry in our hurt and needy society. Love is a central theme of music, art, and literature. Every personal relationship needs love to survive.

In man's search for meaning, however, he most often forgets the only source of true love. The Apostle John defined true love when he wrote, **"In this the love of God was manifested toward us, that God has sent His only begotten Son into the world, that we might live through Him. In this is love, not that we loved God, but that He loved us and sent His Son to be the propitiation** [the satisfaction of the demands of God's justice] **for our sins"** (1 John 4:9-10 NKJV).

God's kind of love is not based on the loveliness or merit of the object. This love is called Αγαπη in the original Greek. It includes His foes as well as His friends. Jesus described αγαπη, **"...love your enemies, bless those who curse you, do good to those who hate you, and pray for those who spitefully use you and persecute you, that you may be sons of your Father in heaven; for He makes His sun rise on the evil and on the good, and sends rain on the just and on the unjust"** (Matthew 5:44 NKJV).

(See also John 3:16; 16:27; Romans 5:8; Ephesians 2:4; 1 John 3:1; 4:9-16.)

FIFTH: GOD IS *ETERNAL LIFE*

There has never been a time when God did not exist, and there never will be a time when He ceases to exist. He is the unmoved Mover, the ground of all being. His existence has no beginning and no end. He is the answer to the question men have grappled with since the dawn of history, "What is the power, the force, the Person who created everything that exists?" He is the self-existent fount of both physical and spiritual life.

What does God say about His eternal nature? **"'I am the Alpha and the Omega, the Beginning and the End,' says the Lord, 'who is and who was and who is to come, the Almighty'"** (Revelation 1:8 NKJV).

His changeless, permanent nature has no beginning and no end. **"Before the mountains were brought forth, or ever You had formed the earth and the world, even from**

everlasting to everlasting, You are God." (Psalm 90:2).
"Jesus Christ is the same, yesterday, today, and forever"
(Hebrews 13:8 NKJV).

Paul broke into praise as He thought of this attribute:
"Who alone posssesses immortality and dwells in unap-
proachable light..." (I Timothy 6:16).

What is true of God the Father is also true of the Son
and the Holy Spirit. They are called the Trinity. "For there
are three that bear witness, the Spirit and the water [the
Father] and the blood [the Son]; and the three are in agreement" (1 John 5:8).

Jesus, in His divine nature, has eternal existance. He
clearly claimed this when His enemies questioned how He
could have known Abraham who lived 2,000 years before: "'I
tell you the truth,' Jesus answered, 'before Abraham was
born, I am!'" (John 8:58 NIV).

(See also Exodus 15:18; Deuteronomy 32:40; 33:27; Job
36:26; Psalm 9:7;1 35:13; Lamentations 5:19; 1 Timothy
1:17; Revelation 1:8.)

SIXTH: GOD IS *OMNISCIENT*

God possesses all the knowledge there is to have.
Nothing takes God by surprise. When we couple His eternity
with omniscience it means that there never was a time when
God did not know all things, whether actual or potential. He
possesses all the knowledge there ever was, is, or will be.

This knowledge extends to even the smallest details.
Jesus said that not even a sparrow can fall to the ground without the Father's knowledge (Matthew 10:29), and that "the
very hairs of your head are all numbered" (v.30). "So thou

shalt not sweat" how God will take care of your problems.

God asserts that omniscience is unique to Him when He challenged the false prophets and occultists through Isaiah, **"'Present your case,' the Lord says. 'Bring forward your strong arguments,' the King of Jacob says, 'Let them bring forth and** *declare to us what is going to take place;* **As for the former events, declare what they were, that we may consider them, and know their outcome; or** *announce to us what is coming.* *Declare the things that are going to come afterward,* **that we may know that you are gods...'"** (Isaiah 41:21-23).

This is why God uses prophecy to validate who is His true messenger. Because only an omniscient God can know and predict the future with one hundred percent accuracy. (See Deuteronomy 18:15-21.)

Often we make poor judgments because we don't have all the facts. But God has access to the total universe of information. He even knows what will be discovered tomorrow. This is why it is stupid for us not to claim His promise, **"Trust in the Lord with all your heart, and lean not on your own understanding; In all your ways acknowledge Him, and He shall direct your paths"** (Proverb 3:5-6 NKJV).

(See also Job 26:6; 31:4; 34:21; Psalm 147:5; Proverbs 15:3; Hebrews 4:13; 1 John 3:20.)

SEVENTH: GOD IS *OMNIPRESENT*

The Creator God is not limited by time and space as we are. Time and space are His creation and He exists in a dimension far above them. He is able to permeate time and space and be personally present everywhere at all times. The Psalmist, David, comforted himself in a time of extreme stress with this wonderful truth, **"Where can I go from your Spirit? Where can I flee from your presence? If I go up to the heavens, you are there; if I make my bed in the depths, you are there. If I rise on the wings of the dawn, if I settle on the far side of the sea, even there your hand will guide me, your right hand will hold me fast"** (Psalm 139:7-10 NIV).

God is a spirit and is personally present in all places at once. Jesus made this clear when He taught a Samaritan woman about *the place* to worship God, **"Jesus declared, 'Believe me, woman, a time is coming when you will worship the Father neither on this mountain nor in Jerusalem... Yet a time is coming and has now come when the true worshipers will worship the Father in spirit and truth, for they are the kind of worshipers the Father seeks. God is spirit, and his worshipers must worship in spirit and in truth"** (John 4:21, 23 -24 NIV). You see, Jesus taught her that worshipping God was not about a certain physical location. Since God is an omnipresent Spirit, He cannot be confined to one place. He is personally present with everyone who truly seeks Him and worships Him in his heart wherever he may be. Jesus anticipated the time when the Law of Moses would be set aside as a way of approaching God, and declared that worship is no longer confined to the Temple in Jerusalem.

The following promises are based on this attribute:

"I am with you and will watch over you wherever you go, and I will bring you back to this land. *I will not leave you* until I have done what I have promised you" (Genesis 28:15 NIV).

"Then the Lord said to Jacob, 'Go back to the land of your fathers and to your relatives, and *I will be with you*'" (Genesis 31:3 NIV).

"Keep your lives free from the love of money and be content with what you have, because God has said, *'Never will I leave you; never will I forsake you'*" (Hebrews 13:5 NIV).

(See also Deuteronomy 4:39; 31:6; Joshua 1:9; Proverbs 15:3; Isaiah 66:1; Jeremiah 23:24; Acts 17:27.)

EIGHTH: GOD IS *OMNIPOTENT*

God is all powerful, having more than enough strength to do the sum total of all things. He has omnipotent power over nature, over the course of history and over human life.

As with all of the attributes, all three members of the Trinity are said to possess them. The Second Person (the Son, Jesus) is in focus in these verses, **"For in Him all things were created, both in the heavens and on earth, visible and invisible, whether thrones or dominions or rulers or authorities — all things have been created through Him and for Him. And He is before all things, and in Him all things hold together"** (Colossians 1:16-17).

Here we see that God the Son's omnipotence not only created all things, but He continues to sustain all things by His almighty power. As Hebrews 1:3 adds, **"He...upholds all things by the word of His power."**

When Job was in great distress he looked up to the Lord believed in His omnipotence, **"I know that You can do everything, and that no purpose of Yours can be withheld from You"** (Job 42:2 NKJV).

I have been asked this question several times, "Could God make a rock so big that He couldn't lift it?" This question is based on a gross ignorance of God's nature. It takes infinitely more power to create a rock out of nothing, than it takes to lift it. So if God can create the rock, He can certainly do the lesser thing of lifting it.

This attribute has been the basis of many great, comforting promises that we can claim today.

When Mary questioned how she, a virgin, could have a son, the angel said, "**...nothing will be impossible with God**" (Luke 1:37).

When Jesus showed how perfect men have to be if they are to be saved by keeping the Law of Moses, "**The disciples...were very astonished and said, 'Then who can be saved?' And looking upon them Jesus said to them, 'With men this is impossible, but** *with God* <u>*all*</u> *things are possible.*'" (Matthew 19:25,26).

Because God has all power, He can and does strengthen us when we believe His promises, "**Do you not know? Have you not heard? The Lord is the everlasting God, the Creator of the ends of the earth. He will not grow tired or weary, and his understanding no one can fathom. He gives strength to the weary and increases the power of the weak**" (Isaiah 40:28-29 NIV).

(See also Job 42:2; 26:7; Psalm 115:3; Matthew 19:26; Mark 14:36; Hebrews 3:6; Revelation 19:6.)

NINTH: GOD IS *IMMUTABLE*

This attribute means that God never changes in His nature or attributes. When He makes a promise or declares a truth, it will never change or not be fulfilled. Therefore we can believe that when He says He will do something, He will do it.

The Bible records more than seven thousand things God promises for His children. And you can trust Him to keep His word. For **"God is not a man, that He should lie, nor a son of man, that He should repent; Has He said, and will He not do it? Or has He spoken, and will He not make it good?"** (Numbers 23:19).

It is comforting to know that we serve a God who does not change His mind, His Word, His nature, His plans, or His actions.

The same God who created the order of the universe still guides the affairs of man. He is constant and reliable. **"The counsel of the Lord stands forever, The plans of His heart from generation to generation"** (Psalm 33:11).

God's immutability guarantees our spiritual gifts and callings, **"For the gifts and the callings of God are irrevocable"** (Romans 11:29 NKJV).

(See also Psalm 33:11; Hebrews 1:12; 13:8.)

TENTH: GOD IS *TRUTH* OR *VERACITY*

God is absolute truth. Anything in word or deed that doesn't conform to what He has revealed in His Word is *not* the truth. To know Him is to know reality.

The Lord is the essence of everything that is valid, authentic and real. **"He is the Rock, His work is perfect; for all His ways are justice, a God of truth and without injustice; righteous and upright is He"** (Deuteronomy 32:4 NKJV).

Jesus said, **"Sanctify them in the truth; Thy word is truth"** (John 17:17).

If something does not conform to what He has revealed in His Word, it is not the truth. **"For the word of the Lord is right, And all His work is done in truth"** (Psalm 33:4).

He's a God of integrity and cannot lie. It is against His very nature.

(See also 2 Samuel 7:28; Psalm 146:6; Isaiah 65:16.)

THE INFINITE GAP

There's not a person who's ever lived who could compare his life with God's character and say, "That's just the kind of person I am."

No, the Bible makes a sober statement about what man is like: **"The heart is deceitful above all things, and desperately wicked..."** and **"All our righteousnesses are like filthy rags"** (Jeremiah 17:9; Isaiah 64:6 NKJV).

It isn't very flattering, is it? Isaiah isn't saying that it's just our *bad* habits and deeds that are offensive to God. It's what we would consider our *good* human acts that offend God as well. He describes them as *filthy* because by comparison with God's holy character they fall so far short.

I know this is hard to swallow, especially for people who have always prided themselves on the good things they do for God and their fellowman. But listen to what the Apostle James says: **"Whoever keeps the whole law and yet stumbles in *one* point, he has become guilty of all** [breaking the whole law]" (James 2:10).

The Apostle Paul says virtually the same thing: **"Cursed is every one who does not abide by *all things* written in the book of the Law, to perform them"** (Galatians 3:10b).

WHAT IS THE LAW?

The Law of God, which is summarized in the Ten Commandments and the Sermon on the Mount, expresses the overwhelming purity of God's holy character. All the laws that God has ever given to men tell us what we'd have to be like if we were to try to approach God on the basis of our own merit.

But according to James and Paul, we could keep every single point of the law and yet stumble in just *one small area* and that would be enough to disqualify us from enjoying fellowship with God for even a moment.

What a commentary on the magnitude of God's holiness!

The reason it's so difficult for us to accept the absoluteness of this concept is because of all the relativistic thinking that predominates our lives. We just can't fathom a holiness that won't bend "just a little" to accommodate our human weaknesses. And none of us can believe that those "little" sins we commit could be so offensive to God.

STATISTICS DON'T LIE!

Of course, once we start trying to decide if one of our sins is a little or a big one, we've got a delicate job on our hands. What we call "little" might not seem that way to God at all.

But suppose that an average person sinned only one "little" sin a day from the age of five, until he was sixty-five years old. By that time he would have on his hands (or should I say "conscience") 21,915 sins.

That means that at least 21,915 times the person fell short of measuring up to the character of God, which is the perfect standard that God measures man against.

But, you say, suppose for every sin that man committed he did five good deeds. Wouldn't that offset his sins and balance the scorecard?

Let me answer that with an illustration.

SINK OR SWIM

The State of Hawaii boasts of one of the most comfortable climates in the entire world. Say that you and I want to take a trip there, but neither of us can afford to go by commercial means. So we decide to swim.

Our plan is to meet at 6:00 A.M. one day and leave from Long Beach, California. Our families come down to the ocean to see us off, someone offers up a prayer for divine guidance (we'll need it!), another man fires a pistol with blanks, and away we go.

By midmorning we're exhausted, and by noon we begin to sink. There is no way we can make it. It is simply beyond human ability. Maybe you go fifteen miles, I go ten, but we still fall hopelessly short of the 2,400-mile distance.

Perhaps an Olympic champion could get in shape for a marathon swim and go one hundred miles. That would be a valiant effort, but it would still be at least 2,300 miles short of Hawaii. We could all stand around and marvel at the grand effort, but the champion would still be dead.

People tend to compare themselves with each other and see who comes the closest to a given mark. But "closeness" doesn't count with God. Coming close counts in darts, horseshoes, and hand grenades, but not in holiness. Interestingly, the root word for sin means "to miss the mark."

What I'm trying to get across is that there is no possible way to achieve right standing with God by our own human efforts. The standard is too tough! There has to be some divine intervention by which man has supernaturally credited to him God's own righteousness.

THE DIVINE DILEMMA

We've seen that a major barrier between God and man is the holy character of God. We owe God perfect obedience to His righteous character. We can't pay. Because all mankind fails to measure up to God's attributes of righteousness and justice, we are all banned from His presence and any relationship with Him. This is called spiritual death.

God told our first parents, Adam and Eve, that if they disobeyed His one command, there would be the awesome consequence of spiritual death immediately, and physical death eventually. When they flaunted God's command and disobeyed, they incurred a DEBT OF SIN with God.

When any law is broken, a "debt to the law" is incurred and justice demands retribution of some kind. So when man broke God's law, the justice of God had to demand full payment — perfect righteousness or death. Man was immediately banished from free access to the intimate presence of his loving Creator.

Now, here was God's dilemma (to illustrate it in human terms). Whereas the *justice* of God burned in wrath against man for outraging His holiness, God's *love* equally yearned to find a way to justly forgive him and bring him back into fellowship with Himself.

But how could God express His *love*, His *righteousness*, and His *justice* toward man all at the same time and not compromise one or the other? How could He not require the justly deserved DEBT OF SIN be paid? There was no greater challenge ever to confront God than how He could remain just and yet declare sinners forgiven and righteous. How could God satisfy the requirements of His absolute righteousness which could not allow anyone less than that into His presence?

Justice and love both had to be vindicated. But how could they be when the righteous demand of justice required that rebellious man be banished forever from God's holy presence?

Can a judge whose son has broken the law do away with the law in order to free his son?

The answer to these questions is the most important information you will ever learn.

CHAPTER 4

BARRIER NUMBER TWO:

A DEBT OF SIN

T o understand the nature of this *debt of sin*, we have to reach back into the practices of the criminal courts of the Roman Empire.

In the days of the great dominion of Rome, all Roman law was built on the assumption that every Roman citizen owed Caesar perfect allegiance and obedience to his laws. Roman justice was enforced swiftly if any citizen broke one of his laws. The offender would soon find himself standing before the courts or Caesar himself.

NAILED TO THE PRISON DOOR

If the man were found guilty of breaking the law and sentenced to prison, an itemized list was made of each infraction and its corresponding penalty. This list was, in essence, a record of how the man had failed to live up to the laws of Caesar. It was technically called a "Certificate of Debt."

When the man was taken to his prison cell, this Certificate of Debt was nailed to his cell door so that anyone passing by could tell that the man had been justly condemned and could also see the limitations of his punishment. For instance, if he were guilty of three crimes and the total time of imprisonment was twenty years, then it would be illegal to keep him there twenty-five years, and all could see that.

When the man had served his time and was released,

he would be handed the yellowed, tattered Certificate of Debt with the words "Paid in Full" written across it. He could never again be imprisoned for those same crimes as long as he could produce his canceled Certificate of Debt.

But until the sentence was paid, that Certificate of Debt stood between him and freedom. It continued to witness to the fact that the imprisoned man had failed to live according to the laws of Rome and was, in essence, an offense to Caesar.

MANKIND'S "CERTIFICATE OF DEBT"

As we saw in the last chapter, man owes God perfect obedience to His holy laws as summarized in the Ten Commandments and the Sermon on the Mount. By his failure to live up to this standard of perfection, man has become an offense to the very character of God, and the eternal court of justice has pronounced the death sentence upon man.

A Certificate of Debt was prepared against every person who would ever live, listing his failure to live in thought, word, and deed in accordance with the law of God. This death sentence has become a DEBT OF SIN which has to be paid, either by man or, if possible, someone qualified to take his place (Colossians 2:14).

And this DEBT OF SIN has become another impossible barrier of the wall that separates God and man.

Now, the subject of "sin" isn't too popular. You can tell a person that he's failed to measure up to the holy character of God, and if he's even halfway honest he'll have to agree to that, because that doesn't make him sound too bad.

But somehow people don't like to be told that they're

sinners, even though they know they commit "little" sins all the time. It's all part of the relativistic thinking that's become a part of our society and has helped us rationalize all our actions.

IT'S NOT THE FAULT OF THE ENVIRONMENT

One look at the evening news report is all we need to confirm the mess that men have made of their lives. We don't have to have a degree in psychology, either, to figure out what makes them do what they do. All we have to do is look inside ourselves and we'll see all kinds of emotions, lusts, drives, and temptations that overpower us from time to time and cause us to do things we know are wrong.

Those actions are what God calls "sins," and they *aren't* caused by our environment. They are caused by our "reaction" to our environment, and that's an *internal* problem which man has.

Listen to how Jesus described man and his sinning: **"That which proceeds *out* of the man, that is what defiles the man. For from *within*, out of the heart of men, proceed the evil thoughts and fornications, thefts, murders, adulteries, deeds of coveting and wickedness, as well as deceit, sensuality, envy, slander, pride and foolishness. All these evil things proceed from *within* and defile the man"** (Mark 7:20-23).

These words of Jesus blow most of secular psychology right out of the ballpark because they show that man's wrong actions don't come primarily from *without*, they come from *within*. Misbehavior is not primarily the result of our environment; it's a problem of the heart.

THE SIN NATURE

In using the word "heart," Jesus is talking about that
inner part of man's being which has in it the "sin nature," or a
disposition toward rebellion against God.

Have you ever done something which was totally stupid and senseless and you said to yourself afterwards, "What
on earth made me do that?" Your better judgment *knew* it was
wrong, but you went ahead anyway. Well, it was your "sin
nature" which prompted you to do it.

The Bible uses the terms "flesh" and "sin" (in the singular) to describe that force within us that is in total rebellion
against God. This "nature" was not in man when God created
him. It entered Adam and Eve the moment they disobeyed
God and He withdrew His spiritual life from them.

STRANGER THAN FICTION

I saw a science-fiction movie once that made me
think of how the sin nature works in us. Men from outer
space landed on earth and captured a number of people. They
implanted tiny electrodes in the back of their heads through
which they could completely control the actions of their victims.

After the spaceships left the earth, their victims
remained here and from all appearances seemed to be just like
they'd always been. However, any time the spacemen wanted
them to kill someone or follow any other command, they simply transmitted this to their victims, who were forced to obey.

Our sin natures work a lot like that. Satan, either
directly or through some subtle temptation that appeals to one
of our senses, gets our sin nature to start rebelling against the

known will of God for us (as expressed in His Word) and the first thing you know, we've given in to it and sinned.[1]

DO WE BECOME SINNERS BECAUSE WE SIN?

Sooner or later most of us get around to wondering, "Do I sin because I'm a sinner, or am I a sinner because I sin?"

Now that isn't a silly question like "Which came first, the chicken or the egg?" It's very important to know whether my sinning stems from a nature with which I'm born, whether it's just something I start doing because everyone else does it, or whether it's "caught" like some disease.

The Bible teaches that when Adam and Eve disobeyed God in the Garden of Eden, they didn't just lose their sense of fellowship with God and become unlike Him in their character; they actually had something *added* to them — a sin nature. And that made them sinners. Since that awful day of infamy, all men have been born with that same sinful nature, and that is the source of our sins.

I know it's hard to believe that a tiny, innocent baby cooing sweetly in our arms has in it a sin nature that will soon begin committing sins, but that's what the Bible teaches from start to finish.

WHEN IS SIN, SIN?

Is it a sin to be tempted?

The answer to that is No. If a girl in a short miniskirt stoops down to pick a flower and I'm standing right behind her, there's no way I can stop a tempting thought from passing through my mind. But if I continue to look and start to toy with the idea of getting into the sack with her, then it becomes a sin.

The sin is not the temptation; the sin is in not saying No to the temptation and in not handing it over to Christ for Him to deal with on the spot.

IT'S WHAT'S INSIDE THAT COUNTS

To me, the greatest thing that true Christianity has to offer is that it starts with the *inside*. The Holy Spirit takes up permanent residence inside of us. He gives us new motivation, new hope, and new power for living. Religion offers an *external* program or code of ethics that seeks to change a man's outer behavior. That would be all right if that was where the problem is, but it's not. This sort of outer renovation usually blinds men to the real problem, which is the unreformable sin nature on the *inside*.

I heard once of a girl who was having terrible stomach pains and went to the doctor for some medicine. He gave her a bottle of green-colored liquid and told her to take two tablespoons internally every three hours. Well, she took one whiff of the medicine and nearly vomited. So she hit upon another plan. She decided to *rub* the two tablespoons *on* her stomach every three hours.

The medicine smelled as bad as it looked and strangely enough, although she was saturated with the medicine, she didn't get any better. Of course, when she went back to the doctor, he quickly convinced her that all the medicine in the world rubbed on the *outside* of her stomach wasn't going to get her well. The problem was on the *inside* and that's where the remedy needed to be applied.

Now, you know, of course, that was only a silly story, but I hope you got the point. The problem that men have is

called "sin," and it's down *inside* of us. No amount of "medicine" applied to the *outside* can ever soak through to where
this problem of sin is.

Jesus addressed this issue of religion when He said to
**the devout religious leaders of His day, "...Now then, you
Pharisees clean the outside of the cup and dish, but inside
you are full of greed and wickedness. You foolish people!
Did not the one who made the outside make the inside
also?"** (Luke 11:39-40 NIV).

Because men can't stand to admit that they have this
internal weakness called sin, they've invented "religion" and
"philosophy." Both these studies more or less admit that
mankind has a problem, but generally speaking, they believe
it's external in nature and can be solved through rituals or reason.

I personally believe it's another case of the old "oint-
ment on the stomach" routine, and although for many a
"patient" the operation appears to be successful, unfortunately
the patient dies.

SUMMING IT UP

In summarizing this barrier to God, man's DEBT OF
SIN, we can see that man's problem is really twofold.

First is the fact that when Adam and Eve sinned, they
died spiritually and lost their relationship and fellowship with
God. In place of spiritual life, a nature of sin and rebellion
against God resulted. Because we can only reproduce what
we are, all of Adam and Eve's children were born with their
condition. This sin nature is the source of all of our "acts" of
sin and is a major reason why we are unacceptable for a relationship with God.

Secondly, a DEBT OF SIN was incurred by them and all mankind. The penalty for that debt is death, and it must be paid either by us or by someone qualified and willing to take our place.

ADAM WASN'T THE ONLY CULPRIT

It makes a lot of people angry to hear that something which some far-off ancestor did implicates them with such grievous consequences. And I can sympathize with how they feel.

But in God's mind, Adam was representative man— the federal head of the human race. What he did judicially implicated all his fellowmen. If the President of the United States and our Congress declared war on some country today, I would be at war too, even though I might not personally be in favor of it. It makes no difference whether I voted for them or not. What they did would implicate me because they act as my federal head.

A story I have heard illustrates this very well.

In the days of slavery, old Mose grew weary of working out in the cotton fields and chopping wood day after day and year after year. One day Mose got to thinking about whose fault it was that his lot in life was so tough. After finding legitimate excuses for everyone he could think of, he finally decided it was all really Adam's fault for eating that forbidden fruit in the first place. That drove man out of his lush, comfortable garden home and into the fields to toil by the sweat of his brow.

The more he thought about this, the angrier Mose got with Adam. As he swung his axe into each block of wood, he'd mutter, "Old Adam, old Adam," whacking a little harder with each utterance.

One day his master came along and overheard this tirade. He went up to Mose and asked him what he meant by "Old Adam."

"Well," said Mose, "if it hadn't been for Adam, I wouldn't be stuck out here in this woodpile, slavin' away all day long. I'd be in the house restin' and sippin' lemonade."

The master thought for a minute and then he said, "You come into the house, Mose. From now on you don't have to do any more hard work. You can lay around all day long, doing whatever you like. There is just one thing, though. See the little box here on the table? I don't want you to ever open it. Okay? Enjoy yourself now."

Well, for the next few weeks Mose couldn't get over his good fortune. He wandered around the house enjoying his leisure and lemonade.

Then he noticed the box the master had spoken about. At first all he did was look at it. But as the days went by, the temptation grew stronger and stronger to touch it. After a few days of only feeling it and carrying it around, it finally got too much for him and he couldn't imagine what harm there'd be in just a little peek into it.

As he cautiously opened one corner of it, a white piece of paper inside caught his eye. His curiosity wouldn't be satisfied until he'd taken out the paper and read it. This is what it said:

"Mose, you old rascal. I don't ever want you to blame Adam again. If you'd been there in the garden, you'd have done the same thing Adam did. Now, you hightail it back out to the woodpile and get to chopping again."

The point of the story is evident. If we'd been in Adam's shoes, we would have done the same thing he did.

God in His great foreknowledge (His omniscience) could see that all men would have, indeed, ratified Adam's rebellion.

But the good news of the "Gospel" is that God so loved the world that, at infinite cost to Himself, He provided a means of removing man's DEBT OF SIN and of dealing with the nature of sin in men.

---

1. For a full explanation of how this principle of rebellion to the Law works, see the author's book, *Satan Is Alive and Well on Planet Earth,* chapter 12, "The Guilt Trip" (Grand Rapids: Zondervan Publishing House, 1972).

CHAPTER 5

BARRIER NUMBER THREE:

SLAVERY TO SATAN

U p to now we have dealt with two of the basic problems that help form the barrier that exists between God and man. We have seen how man's sin was an affront to the holy CHARACTER OF GOD, and how his failure to keep God's laws resulted in a DEBT OF SIN.

Now let's take a look at the third great barrier separating God and man, the fact that man is a SLAVE OF SATAN.

I know this assertion will raise bristles with many people, because Jesus got the same reaction when He told some of *His* generation that Satan was their father.

TRUTH IS OFTEN UNPOPULAR

During the early part of His ministry Jesus got into frequent debates with the religious Jews. On one occasion He was talking with a group of militant devotees of Rabbinic Judaism who maintained that because they were born of the seed of Abraham, they were automatically in God's family and God was their Father.

Here is an excerpt of the debate, "Abraham is our father," they answered. **"'If you were Abraham's children,' said Jesus, 'then you would do the things Abraham did. As it is, you are determined to kill me, a man who has told you the truth that I heard from God. Abraham did not do such things. You are doing the things your own father does.' 'We are not illegitimate children,' they protested. 'The only Father we have is God himself.' Jesus said to them, 'If God were your Father, you would love me, for I**

came from God and now am here. I have not come on my
own; but he sent me. Why is my language not clear to
you? Because you are unable to hear what I say'" (John
8:39-43 NIV).

Then Jesus answered His own question as to why
they couldn't understand what He said. **"You belong to your
father, the devil, and you want to carry out your father's
desire. He was a murderer from the beginning, not holding to the truth, for there is no truth in him. When he lies,
he speaks his native language, for he is a liar and the
father of lies. Yet because I tell the truth, you do not
believe me! Can any of you prove me guilty of sin? If I
am telling the truth, why don't you believe me? He who
belongs to God hears what God says. The reason you do
not hear is that you do not belong to God"** (John 8:44-47
NIV).

Needless to say, the reaction Jesus got to this scathing
indictment wasn't too favorable. In fact, after calling Him the
two dirtiest names they could think of — *Samaritan* (a hated
half-breed Jew) and *demon possessed* — they insinuated that
He was the product of an illegitimate birth. Then to top it off,
they tried to stone Him to death, but He slipped out of their
hands.

THE TWO "FATHERHOODS" OF MANKIND

What were the grounds Jesus had for telling His fellow Jews that they were children of Satan?

There were two prime factors.

First, the Jews prided themselves on being children of
Abraham by physical descent and therefore children of God
as a result. Jesus didn't dispute their claim to physical rela-

tionship with Abraham, but He emphatically denied that it made them children of *God*. He told them that unless they had the same faith in Him, as Messiah, which Abraham had had, then Abraham's God wasn't their father, Satan was.

The second point Jesus sought to hammer home was that there are only *two* fatherhoods of mankind, the father-hood of God and the fatherhood of Satan. So, if they weren't God's children, then they must have been Satan's.

That statement drove these "holier than thou" religious leaders into a murderous fury. This issue still affects religious people the same way today. But there's a reason why there's such a violent reaction to this truth. It's because one of Satan's chief tactics down through the history of mankind has been to blur and confuse people with religion.

The first murder in history was committed because Cain was furious that God accepted Abel's offering and not his. Abel presented God with a blood sacrifice for his sin, which was given in obedience to God's previous instructions. Cain brought the work of His own hands, which was the first offering of religion. He was furious when God rejected that which depended on his own effort and merit. So, in a self-righteous rage he killed his brother. Religion hates competi-tion, especially when it exposes man's lack of merit and acceptability to God.

How successful Satan has been in this area is evi-denced by the number of religions, including false Christianity, which have as a basic tenet of their religion that man can do something to earn God's acceptance. They are blind to the impossible barriers that separate all men from God.

Satan also loves to deceive mankind with the idea that we are all children of God and that God is the Father of all. God is the Creator of all mankind, but only the Father of those who have been born spiritually through faith in His Son, the Lord Jesus, the Messiah.

When man was created, he *did* have God's spiritual life resident within him, but when he sinned and turned his back on God, he lost that spiritual life. Now every man is born without it, and if he wants God to be his father for now and through eternity, he must have God's life put back into him sometime before he dies physically on this earth.

A POWERFUL ADVERSARY

How did Satan get to be the powerful authority he seems to be? That he does have power, there is no doubt. History is strewn with the wreckage he's made of individuals and nations.

A classic example of the evil that just one man could do when brought under Satan's *direct* control is the career of Adolf Hitler. There is ample evidence that he was either demon-possessed or possessed by Satan himself.

But damage as great as that is caused every day in this world by a system of thinking and acting which is subtly controlled by Satan to exclude the need for God. The toll in human suffering, physically, emotionally, and spiritually from a lack of a true relationship with God, is incalculable. Broken homes, suicides, murders, rape, greed, hate—all these and more are mute testimony to the fact that this world couldn't possibly be the way God had originally planned it to be.

What went wrong?

ADAM'S POWER-OF-ATTORNEY

In the Genesis account we are told that God put man on earth and entrusted him with authority over himself and all of God's creation. Man was told by God to be fruitful and multiply and replenish, subdue and have dominion over every living thing that moved on the earth (Genesis 1:28).

In other words, God put Adam in charge of this planet and its inhabitants. And aside from the one restraint that God gave him, not to eat of the Tree of the Knowledge of Good and Evil, no other stipulations were laid down as to how he was to govern God's creation.

God actually entrusted Adam with authority over this planet and all that is in it, including himself. He in legal fact had the power-of-attorney to act as God's Vice-regent over Planet Earth.

A WOLF IN SNAKE'S CLOTHING!

But into this paradise came an extra-terrestrial being of superhuman powers. This "Angel of Light" had already brought rebellion into heaven and led a third of all angels into evil with him. Now he intended to spread the rebellion and extend his evil empire to these new creatures of God called human beings.[1]

The name of this being was Lucifer (later known as Satan or the Devil). He was power mad! More than anything else, he wanted to control what God had created and to make himself like God.

So there he was in the Garden. And through his subtle lies and innuendoes about God, he convinced Adam and Eve that they wouldn't die if they ate of the forbidden tree. He said God was holding out on them because He didn't want anyone to be equal with Him. And since this particular tree would give them the knowledge of good and evil, making them as wise as God, they would become like Him.

We look back at that scene now and see the paradise they were enjoying. Then we look at the mess the world is in today and we say, "Wow! They didn't know how good they

had it. How on earth could they have blown it so badly and
felt that God was holding out on them? They literally had
every conceivable thing to make them happy and fulfilled."

The answer should send a chill down our spine.
Satan is able to blind us to all the blessings God has given us,
and to so focus us on the thing we are not supposed to have,
that we throw away everything to get it.

MANKIND'S BENEDICT ARNOLD!

If only Adam and Eve had realized the devastating
consequences that would result from their disobedience to
God's one prohibition.

Not only did they lose their spiritual life and ability to
have free access into the presence and fellowship of God, but
in capitulating to Satan's temptation they unwittingly turned
over their God-given power and authority to Satan's control.
He became the legal controller of all men who would ever be
born from Adam's seed. He also took control of the planet
itself and all creation on it, animal and vegetable.

"But," you may be saying, "how could God permit
such a terrible thing to happen? Couldn't He have taken the
power away from Satan once he'd gotten it from Adam?"

No, He couldn't. You see, God is so just in His
nature that He couldn't even be unjust to Satan. A legal trans-
ference of property and authority had taken place, and the
legal means for reversing it would have to take place *on
another tree.*

THE SLAVE MARKET OF SIN

This sellout of Adam to Satan is how the world got
into the mess it's in today. With Satan as the legal ruler of
this planet, it became one great big slave market and everyone

born into it of Adam's seed is born a slave of Satan.

This was clearly taught by Jesus and His disciples.

The Apostle John wrote, **"The whole world lies in the power of the evil one"** (1 John 5:19b). The word "world" in that verse is the Greek word, *cosmos*, which means an orderly system. This is what is meant when we say that Satan calls the shots over this present world system.

The great defender of the faith, Paul, called Satan **"the god of this world"** and said he had **"blinded the minds of the unbelieving, that they might not see the light of the gospel of the glory of Christ, who is the image of God"** (2 Corinthians 4:4).

In another place in the New Testament Paul spoke of Satan as **"the prince of the power of the air"** and called him **"the spirit that is now working in the sons of disobedience"** (Ephesians 2:1-3).

When the Apostle Paul stood on trial before King Agrippa to defend the message he had been preaching, he clearly declared man's need of being set free from SLAVERY TO SATAN when he said, ''[Jesus sent me] **to open their eyes so that they may turn from darkness to light and** *from the dominion of Satan to God...*'' (Acts 26:18).

JESUS' TEMPTATIONS

The most arrogant display of Satan's authority is seen in his attempt to get Jesus to sin.

You see, Jesus is the only person ever born into this world who was not born under Satan's dominion. The reason is that Jesus did not have a human father, and therefore the curse of SLAVERY TO SATAN which was passed from Adam to all his descendants didn't affect Him.

Jesus was called the **"second Adam"** because He was

the second man who was brought into this world perfect (1 Corinthians 15:45). In His human nature, He could have sinned, just as the first Adam had done. But had He done so He would have been brought under Satan's dominion, just as Adam had been.

Because He was the only person ever born into this world who wasn't a slave to Satan, He became the special object of Satan's hatred. He sought continually either to kill Jesus before He could go to the cross, or get Him to sin so that He would be disqualified to die for sinners.

That's why on one occasion when Satan was tempting Jesus, he showed Him all the kingdoms of the world and their glory and then he said to Him, **"I will give you all this domain and its glory; for it has been handed over to me, and I can give it to whomever I wish. Therefore if You worship before me, it shall all be Yours"** (Luke 4:6,7).

NO CROWN WITHOUT A CROSS

Jesus didn't dispute Satan's claim for a moment. He knew that the world and mankind had been legally transferred by Adam to Satan. He also knew He could take it back from Satan anytime He chose to. But had He done so, it would have meant bypassing the cross. And only at the cross could God pay the ransom price to free enslaved mankind and restore the rightful rulership of the world without compromising His justice.

For Him to have chosen the easy way and taken the crown of dominion from Satan would have been against His divine nature. And the instant He obeyed Satan, He, too, would have entered into the slave market of sin and come under Satan's control.

Consequently there would have been no "free man" in the world who could pay the ransom price and set men free from their bondage to Satan. All would have been in the slave market together, and none could have qualified to buy anyone else's freedom.

SATAN IS "SOME" FATHER!

At the beginning of this chapter we talked about a conversation Jesus had with some unbelieving Jews and how He had told them that Satan was their father.

When you think of someone as being a "father," you usually picture some kindly, concerned, and tenderhearted person who has his children's best interests at heart.

But, though Satan knows how to masquerade as an "angel of light," his heart is black and evil, full of hate and bitter revenge against God and men. This is no normal father. This is an evil, sadistic creature who has imprisoned his children in a slave camp, caring nothing for them as human beings. He uses them for his purposes and then throws them on a junk heap when he's finished with them.

Satan's great worry is that when mankind finds out a ransom has been paid for their freedom, they no longer need to be his slave.

But until they find this out, man's SLAVERY TO SATAN is a barrier to a restored fellowship with God, the heavenly Father.

---

1. For a fuller understanding of Satan, his origin, and his fall, read the author's book, *Satan Is Alive and Well on Planet Earth* (Grand Rapids: Zondervan Publishing House, 1972).

CHAPTER 6

BARRIER NUMBER FOUR:

SPIRITUAL DEATH

A friend told me a story once that illustrates clearly what it's like to be spiritually dead.

He said his son had gotten an electric train for Christmas and together the two of them got it all set up. They spent hours playing with it, and the train raced up and down the tracks through the tunnels and in and out of the depot.

One day when he came home from work, his son met him at the door and was really upset: the train wouldn't run. Together they took the electrical mechanisms apart, but they all checked out fine. They checked the connections between all the cars, and they were all in place.

After hours of trying to get the train running they were baffled. There was no power getting through to the train. For all practical purposes it was dead.

Then, by chance, my friend spotted a small metal crossing sign that had fallen across the tracks and was obscured by some buildings along the rails. As he picked up the crossing sign from the tracks, the train began to roll.

What had happened was that the metal on the tracks had caused a short circuit. All the power of the City of Los Angeles was kept from entering that train because of a tiny piece of seemingly insignificant metal.

MANKIND IS "SHORT-CIRCUITED"

As we've looked at in previous chapters, there was a
time when God and man experienced an unbroken fellowship
and things were fine between them. Then something happened that short-circuited the relationship between God and
man. Something fell across mankind's "tracks," and all the
divine power and spiritual life of the omnipotent Creator God
were cut off from His special creation, man, and he became
dead spiritually.

That "something" was sin!

It's not as though this awful consequence took Adam
and Eve by surprise. God had told them that the day they ate
of the Tree of the Knowledge of Good and Evil, they would
die (Genesis 2:17). But since they had never seen anything
die before, they didn't fully comprehend what "death" meant.

THE THREE FACES OF DEATH

Adam and Eve had no idea how utterly disastrous it
would be to be *spiritually dead* in relationship to their wonderful Creator. Likewise they didn't comprehend the horror of
eventually being cut off from each other and their loved ones
by *physical death*. And finally, they failed completely to realize the implications of *eternal death*, that condition of separation from God for eternity.

Although all three aspects of this death sentence
imposed upon them went into effect immediately, only one
was instantly evident to man himself. He knew that something irreparable had happened to his rapport with God.

That "something" was SPIRITUAL DEATH.

Adam and Eve immediately felt an alienation from

God and even went so far as to hide themselves from Him. But even though God went looking for them and, by His gracious words and actions, reassured them of His love, He nevertheless had to execute the sentence of death and separate them from fellowship. Hence Adam was banished from the garden and free access to God.

THE "SIN" INFECTION

Sin and death had entered the human race through one man's disobedience (Romans 5:12). When Adam sinned he *became* a sinner, and that one sin infected the whole human race, still in his loins, with the sickness of sin and death. Since then, all men are *born* sinners with the sentence of death upon them.

A LOOK AT MAN FROM GOD'S VIEWPOINT

There's no way to even begin to understand how that event in the Garden affected mankind down through the centuries and even today, until we get a look at God as He really is, and ourselves as He sees us.

In creating man, God anticipated every physical and mental faculty that man would ever need to relate to the beautiful material world into which He placed him.

However, God also equipped man to function in relation to the nonphysical or spiritual realm which is even more real. He did so by giving man a soul and a spirit.

The following diagram gives you a picture of how the three parts of man's make-up work together. When seeking to express divine truth, no human illustration is perfect, but this

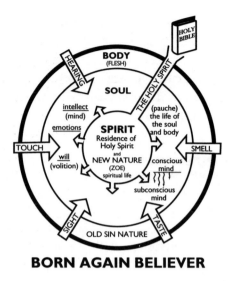

BORN AGAIN BELIEVER

diagram suffices to give us the framework we need for looking at the interwoven and sometimes separate functions of the body, soul, and spirit of man.

THE BODY

The body is the *material* part of man, that part which enables him to function in and relate to the physical world around him. The body contains physical life. This is an elusive, indefinable force which keeps the heart beating. Despite the various efforts to create human life, no one has succeeded in creating and sustaining the kind of life necessary to cause a human body to function as designed.

When the body dies, it returns to the dust it was taken from. But that's not the end of it. Eventually it will be brought back together again and have an eternal existence, either with God or separated from Him.

THE SOUL

The soul is the immaterial part of man. When God formed man, He breathed into man's nostrils the breath of *lives* and man became a living soul (Genesis 2:7). The Hebrew word translated "life" in most English versions of the Bible should actually have been translated "lives" because it's a plural word in the original Hebrew Bible.

I believe it was no accident that the Bible says God breathed into man "lives" instead of "life," because all through the rest of the Bible two kinds of life are spoken of in relation to man — soulish life and spiritual life.

'The soulish life contains the image of God in man. Being in the image of God means that man, like God, has intellect, emotion, moral reasoning, volition, and eternity of being. It does not refer to us "looking" like God physically, however, or having His *spiritual* life in us.

Physical life and soulish life are one and the same. For, if you take the physical life from a man, his soul also departs from his body. And if you take the soul out of a man, it means he is dead physically. Even though a person may live for many years in a state of deep unconsciousness, it doesn't mean his soul has left him. It's simply that his physical body will not respond to the impulses sent to it from his soul.

The five senses located in the physical body are the windows of the soul. They're the means of bringing the information about the physical world into the mind of man. But their limitation is that they can't substantiate reality which is outside the physical realm.

For instance, the rationality that much of the world has is that if it can't be seen, tasted, touched, smelled, or heard, it isn't real. This approach to life is usually called "materialistic" or "empiricist." The problem with this philosophy is that it shuts out a whole realm of existence that's outside the world of the senses.

This is the realm of the spirit.

THE SPIRIT

When God breathed into man the breath of lives, not only did He give him soulish or physical life, but He also gave man God's own kind of life — spiritual life.

You see, God is spirit and in order to worship Him the proper way, or fellowship with Him on a personal basis, we must have the same kind of life — spiritual life (John 4:24).

That's why God created man with a human spirit. It was to be the part of man to contain God's spiritual life. Adam and Eve had soulish life *and* spiritual life. With their soulish life they comprehended the beauty of their physical surroundings and each other. With their spiritual life they experienced communication with God who was present in the Garden as a spirit.

You might say that man was originally created with *six* senses instead of five. Five of them plugged him in to the physical world and operate on *soulish* power. The sixth sense, which is called "faith," operates on *spiritual* power. It enabled him to establish reality in the spiritual realm and experience uninhibited communication with God.

THE TRAGEDY OF THE FALL

Aside from all the other disastrous consequences of man's disobedience to God, perhaps the worst is that God withdrew from man His spiritual life and left man with a dead spirit, a spiritual vacuum if you please. No longer did man have the internal spiritual equipment to experience a relationship with God who is a spirit. Within a few generations of Adam, men had so lost their concept of the one true God that they wandered hopelessly in spiritual darkness.

You can see the dilemma that arose between God and man. Whereas God had made man in such a way that communication with him would be possible through his spirit, now that man no longer had spiritual life. So God had to communicate with men in ways that their five senses could comprehend.

That's the whole story of the Bible: God seeking ways to make fallen man aware of His existence, His love, and His judgment against sin. But always God had to take the initiative and reach out to man in ways that he could understand by sight, hearing, taste, touch, or smell.

THE BARRIER IS COMPLETE

So here we have the complete picture of the universal barrier which separates man from God. Man can't tear the barrier down and he can't climb over it by his own efforts. In fact, he can't even climb over with God's help. The barrier must come down, and God alone can do that.

You will meet people every day who say they have no need for God and don't feel any of the barriers we've looked at. But the crucial issue is that God says they have a need whether they are aware of that need or not. And His Word shows very clearly what the need is.

I may visit the doctor, and he could say to me, "Hal, you have a severe illness which proper treatment can completely cure."

"But, Doc, I don't *feel* sick."

"No matter. Tests show conclusively that you're ill."

Since he's an expert in his field, I really have little choice but to take his word for it. After all, effective cure depends completely on accurate diagnosis. But after the diagnosis is made, I've got to submit myself to the cure.

God says we have a problem. That problem is called sin. It's a fatal disease with only one known cure. Let's take a look now at what that remedy is.

CHAPTER 7

WHY GOD HAD TO BECOME A MAN

Have you ever stopped to wonder what the main factor is that divides true Christianity and most other religions?

Christians accept the same God of the Old Testament that Jews and several other religions do. But where they part company with other creeds is that in the Christian teaching the God of the Old Testament actually put on a human body for thirty-three years, and without ceasing to be God, He lived on this earth as a true man.

To many religions, and the Jews especially, this concept is blasphemy. But in true Christianity, this conviction that God took on human form is so central that unless it's true, there is no adequate explanation as to how the barriers that separate God and man could be torn down.

Furthermore, Christians believe that the Old Testament gave ample testimony to the fact that God would one day take on a true human nature in His plan to redeem mankind and bring about a reconciliation between Himself and man.

But before we look at who this God-man might be, let's see why it would have been necessary for God to have become a man.

THE GREAT COMMUNICATION GAP

We're very conscious of the communication problems in our modern world. Marriage counselors tell us that the failure to communicate is one of the main factors in couples not being able to reconcile differences. Parents and children grow apart because of this problem.

But as bad as these communication failures are, the greatest breakdown in this area is between God and man.

We've already seen to some extent why this is so. The most basic reason is because God is a spirit and can only be understood in a personal sense by one who also has spiritual life. Men are born with soulish life which gives them a world-consciousness, but they lack spiritual life by which alone they can communicate with God.

Therefore, since the fall of man, God has had to take into account man's inability to comprehend Him both as a person or a spiritual truth. He has been forced to reveal Himself to men in ways that they could understand with their soulish life and their five senses. But it was always with a view to bringing them to a point of faith in His provision for forgiveness of sin.

A NATURALISTS' DILEMMA

His problem was similar to that of the naturalist who had a special concern for a certain ant hill which he had been observing for months. Each day the man spent hours watching the intricate maneuverings of these ants and had come to the place where he felt a very special affinity for them.

One day the naturalist saw a huge bulldozer in the distance and immediately realized that this ant hill lay right in the path of the construction of a new road.

The man panicked. He desperately searched his mind for a way to remove the ants. He scooped up handfuls of them, but they only bit him. He thought of building a fence around the ant pile, but realized the bulldozer would only tear it down.

In his frenzied mind he thought to himself, "If only I could speak to them and tell them about the danger ahead of them. If only I could make them see that I'm their friend and only want to save them from destruction."

But despite his great concern, he could think of no way to communicate to them in a way they would understand. To be able to do that, he'd have to become an ant himself, and yet retain the nature of a man so he could continue to clearly assess the problem and make it known to the ants.

GOD'S HUMAN "ANT HILL"

Down through the long history of the human race, God has spared no effort to reveal Himself to man in terms of natural and material phenomena which man could comprehend.

David, the Psalmist, tells us that the whole world is God's "kindergarten" to teach us the ABCs of the reality of God and the spiritual realm.

The Spirit of God declared through David, **"The heavens are telling of the glory of God; And the firmament** [earth] **is declaring the work of His hands. Day to day pours forth speech, and night to night reveals knowledge. There is no speech, nor are there words; their voice is not heard. Their line** [sound] **has gone out through all the earth, and their utterances to the end of the world"** (Psalm 19:1-4a).

This is one of the most profound things ever said in the Bible. It tells us that the great majesty and marvel of the universe with its heavenly bodies — the beauty, the wonder and the incredible balance of design and function of all the creation of God on the earth — are the actual verbalization of the fact that there is an Almighty, Infinite God Whose hands created them all.

The fact that day follows day with such certainty and night after night appears like clockwork is the same as God actually speaking to man about His reality and trustworthiness.

The original Hebrew of the above Scripture literally says, **"They aren't actually speaking nor can you listen intently and hear any words as such, but nevertheless, their sound has gone out to all the earth."**

Why the Sound?

What's the purpose of this grandiose demonstration in nature of the reality of God?

"WHAT ABOUT THE HEATHEN IN AFRICA?"

The Apostle Paul in the New Testament gives us the answer to that question — and in the process answers why the heathen in Africa, or any other remote place, is held accountable to seek the true God.

"That which is known about God is evident within them [men]; for God made it evident to them. For since the creation of the world His invisible attributes, His eternal power and divine nature, have been clearly seen, being understood through what has been made, so that they are without excuse" (Romans 1:19, 20).

Paul says the true nature of the invisible God has been openly revealed by His material creation so that the soulish intellects of men could put two and two together and come up with the realization that God exists.

But not only to recognize that He exists. They also are without excuse for not knowing that He will eventually judge ungodliness and the suppression of the truth, and that He is the sovereign authority over men (Romans 1:18).

NATURE'S LESSON IGNORED

It's fairly obvious to a fair-minded thinker that most people down through the history of mankind did not conclude from nature's lesson that there was only one true God, that they were answerable to Him, and that they should above all else seek to know Him.

There's no question but what all civilizations had a concept of some supreme force that wasn't completely controllable by them. And there is abundant evidence in archaeology that men had gods and worshipped them.

But the Apostle Paul tells us their problem. Even though men knew from nature there was a creator God, they didn't honor Him as sovereign in their own lives, but went about daily living as though He had no say-so over them.

Then they would sit around and make futile speculations about what He looked like, where He lived, was He married, did He have children, was He kind and benevolent or harsh and cruel. Eventually men ended up making some kind of an image or statue of one of God's creations and worshipped it (see Romans 1:21-25).

Since men were spiritually dead, they could not understand fully what God was like. Yet mankind did have enough light given through nature to reach out to this Creator God and submit themselves to Him. Wherever and whenever in history a human being did do this, the Spirit of God imparted spiritual life to their dead human spirits and they became

children of God. Acts 17:26, 27 brings this out clearly. It
teaches if men so much as *blindly grope* for God, they will
find Him, because He is not far from any one of us.

INTO THE ARENA OF HUMANITY

As powerful as God's nature lesson has been, it was
never intended as God's ultimate revelation of Himself to
man. The only way for God, Who is a Spirit, to fully do and
say what He wanted to mankind, was to actually leave His
eternal residence and enter the arena of humanity.

Even then God wouldn't be able to communicate
with man, who is strictly a physical creature, unless He also
took on physical form and life. But it would also be necessary for Him to retain His divine nature and intellect, or else
He wouldn't be able to accomplish what He'd come to earth
to say and do.

And from the standpoint of God's infinite nature, it
was impossible for The Second Person to cease being God.

THE BARRIERS HAD TO GO!

But what was the main necessity for God to come to
earth?

It was to tear down the barriers that man had erected
between himself and God. No one but God Himself was
capable of doing that job. The obstacles that separated
mankind from God were just too great for a mere human to
overcome.

Some have reasoned that God could have stayed in
heaven and directed men in how to remove the barriers. This
is the "God-helps-those-who-help-themselves" plan.

No! Man could never remove the barriers that separate him from God even with His help. There was no conceivable scenario that involved man's efforts that could satisfy the demands of God's holy character, because the standard by which those efforts had to be measured was God's perfect righteousness.

WHEN ETERNITY STEPPED INTO TIME

Apart from God coming to the rescue, mankind's situation could be summed up in one word: "hopeless." For a holy God who had an unquenchable love for man and a divine necessity to vindicate His justice, the only solution was to leave the glory of heaven, take on flesh and blood, and enter the human race. Since He is the supreme sovereign of the universe, this in no way tainted His deity. God could take on any form He wanted, and it wouldn't have affected who He was intrinsically.

GOD'S PROVISION FOR FORGIVENESS

Remember in the account of the temptation of Adam and Eve, after they had sewn fig leaves together in an effort to hide from God their shame of transgression, God rejected that clothing and took the skins of some animals and clothed them. If you think about it for a minute, the death of those animals is the first record of any creature dying physically.

The animals had done nothing worthy of death, but in their dying a pattern was established by God — an innocent substitute of God's choosing had to give its life, as evidenced by the shed blood, and thereby provide a temporary forgiveness and covering for man's sin.

Several hundred years later when God gave His Law to Moses, He established an inviolate statute, **"Without the shedding of blood there is no remission of sin"** (Hebrews 9:22 paraphrased).

That was the basis of the whole Jewish system of animal sacrifice — an innocent substitute could bear the sin and death penalty due man if the sacrifice was offered to God in accordance with His ordained system of sacrifice and with expectant faith in His forgiveness.

BUT WHY BECOME A MAN?

God revealed through the Prophet Jeremiah that the Law of Moses Covenant was a temporary one when He spoke of a future *New Covenant* that He would establish with Israel. In this He also declared that the animal sacrifice system couldn't go on forever because it provided only a temporary covering for man's sin.

This is the basis of why the writer of the letter to the Hebrews said, **"It is impossible for the blood of bulls and goats to take away sins."** And then he added, **"Every priest stands daily ministering and offering time after time the same sacrifices, which can never take away sins"** (Hebrews 10:4,11). You see, animal sacrifice never took sins away; it merely covered them temporarily from God's judgment. In fact, the root meaning of the Hebrew word *kapar* — translated "atonement" throughout the Old Testament, meant "to cover or hide."

The whole picture God wanted people to understand from the animal sacrifices was that His justice demanded an innocent substitute to take the penalty of death which was due man because of his sin. The fact that God did not exact the death penalty from man, but provided a substitute to die in man's place, was designed to demonstrate to man the greatness of His grace.

But God never planned that His forgiveness would go on being temporary and conditional. From the moment of man's Fall in the Garden, God had in mind a plan that would provide a permanent forgiveness of sin. He planned from the beginning to destroy completely the barriers that separated man from Him.

I'm sure this is why John the Baptist, when he first understood that Jesus was the Messiah, ecstatically proclaimed, **"Behold, the Lamb of God who *takes away* the sin of the world"** (John 1:29). John understood the infinte difference between the animal sacrifices that covered sin temporarily out of sight for Israel, and Jesus, who would *take away forever* the sin of the world as a barrier to relationship with God.

THE FOUNDATION OF GRACE

Since it was human beings who had sinned and incurred the penalty of spiritual and physical death, another true human being would have to be God's final and permanent substitute for man. It would have to be someone of God's choosing who could qualify to step in as a substitute and take the compounded wrath of God against all sin that would ever be committed. The covering for sin provided by the animal sacrifices never included all the sins of a man. And, of course, it made no provision for men who didn't participate in this ritual.

But in order for a man to qualify to take man's place of judgment and be his sin-bearer, there are five things that would have to be true of him:

First, he would have to be a true human being, born into this world the same way other men are. He would have to live and die in the same manner all humans do.

Second, he would have to be without any personal sin of his own for which he would already be under God's condemnation. He would have to be born without a sin nature just as Adam was created without one. At no time in his life could he ever commit even one sin, and yet, he would have to be tested by real temptations.

Third, he would have to live under God's law and keep it perfectly. He would have to be absolutely righteous in his nature and in all his actions so that God's holy character would be satisfied. Therefore, he would have to never break God's law even once in motive, act, or word.

Fourth, he would have to have full knowledge of what he was doing.

Fifth, he would have to be willing to take mankind's guilt as his own and be judged and put to death in the place of all mankind.

WHAT MAN IS THIS?

One of the central reasons for writing this book is to set forth the fact that just such a person came into the world, according to specific predictions and promises, two thousand years ago. He perfectly fulfilled every qualification to be the savior of men.

That man was called Jesus of Nazareth, the Son of the Living God — both the Messiah to Israel, and the Savior of all mankind.

CHAPTER 8

THE MAN THAT GOD BECAME

One of the things that has made the Old Testament scriptures so enduring and always relevant is their prophetic emphasis. Not only was history accurately recorded for us, but hundreds of predictions of future things were made. Unlike prophecy from other sources, the Bible's predictions enjoy a 100% accuracy record in history.

Many of these prophecies had to do with the appearance in Israel of a greater son of David who would be called the Anointed King from God, or the King-Messiah. He alone would bring a kingdom of peace on earth and rule it with righteousness and justice.

There were perhaps hundreds of zealous reformers who appeared on the stage of Israel's history, seeking to fulfill the messianic commission of establishing a kingdom of God on earth. Most of them passed from the scene with little notice or remembrance.

But one such man did not!

It can be clearly demonstrated that some three hundred of the prophecies about the Messiah actually found literal fulfillment in the birth, life, and death of Jesus of Nazareth. The chances of this happening by mere coincidence are mathematically so staggering that it's impossible to calculate.

THE WITNESS OF BIBLE PROPHECY

As you put together the pieces of prophecy in the Old Testament concerning the Messiah, it becomes clear that

ais promised Messiah would be both God and
, is evident from the number of times the prophecies
to Him as a "child" or "son" who would be born.
Then, ften in the same context, it spoke of Him as also being
the Eternal and Almighty God.

Let's look at some of these well-known Old
Testament prophecies.

THE VIRGIN BIRTH

Isaiah 7:14 says, **"Therefore the Lord Himself will
give you a sign: Behold, a virgin will be with child and
bear a son, and she will call His name Immanuel."** The
word "Immanuel" in Hebrew means "God with us."

I'm aware of the efforts of some Bible interpreters to
dismiss this as a prophecy that found its fulfillment in Jesus'
virgin birth. They point out that the Hebrew word *alma* used
for "virgin" can also be translated "young woman."

It's true that it can be translated that way. This is one
of the many "double reference" prophecies in the Old
Testament. It made both a near and a far prediction.

THE GREEK CONNECTION

One of the biggest arguments that the Hebrew scholars understood that it had a far to the future fulfillment and
that this would involve *a virgin* having a son is the translation
they did of the Old Testament into Greek. This translation,
known as the Septaugint, was completed over 160 years
before Jesus was born. The brilliant Hebrew scholars who
made this translation translated the Hebrew word *alma* into
the Greek word παρθενοζ. This Greek word can only mean
virgin.

So, many years before Jesus was born, it was clearly understood that a virgin would bear a son who would be known as, **"God is with us."**

A SON OF DAVID CALLED "GOD"

Isaiah also wrote these clearly prophetic words: **"For unto us a Child is born, unto us a Son is given; and the government will be upon His shoulder. And His name will be called Wonderful, Counselor, *mighty God,* Everlasting Father, Prince of Peace. Of the increase of His government and peace there will be no end, upon the throne of David and over His kingdom, to order it and establish it with judgment and justice from that time forward, even forever"** (Isaiah 9:6,7 NKJV).

Isaiah was not talking about a "spirit" or a heavenly being. The prophecy is clear that the God of Israel would assume a human body and be born into this world like any other man, for it says "a child would be born and a son would be given to Israel." This child is identified as the son of David who would establish his throne forever. Thus it could only be the Messiah.

But even more amazing are the titles given to this child who would be born as a human descendant of David. The antecedant of **"the Mighty God"** is **"the Child"** who would be born and **"the Son"** who would be given to Israel. No prophet of Israel under the inspiration of the Holy Spirit would ever give the title *"El Gibor"* — "Mighty God" — to a mere man. It would have been blasphemy — unless the Lord was revealing that the Messiah would be both man and God miraculously joined together in one person. And such was the inescapable meaning of this prophecy, which also literally calls Him **"the Father of eternity"** and **"the Prince of Peace."** Isaiah passed the test of a true prophet and his word stood in spite of this difficult revelation.

MESSIAH'S BIRTHPLACE PREDICTED

Even the *location* of the Messiah's birth was foretold. More than seven hundred years before God stepped out of eternity into time, Micah the prophet, a contemporary of Isaiah, proclaimed that the Messiah would be born in Bethlehem. He said of this small obscure village in Judea, **"But you, O Bethlehem — the least among the thousands of villages of Judah — out of you shall come forth to me the One who is born to rule over Israel; Whose existence has been from of ancient times — from the days of eternity"** (Micah 5:2).

AN UNWELCOME SURPRISE ANNOUNCEMENT

This prophecy concerning the Messiah was well known among the religious leaders of Israel. However, at the time of Jesus' birth a very startling thing happened. Chaldean court astrologers from Babylon came to Jerusalem and asked, **"Where is He who has been born King of the Jews?"** (Matthew 2:2). They had seen His star in the East and had come to worship Him.

These men were from the same group of which Daniel had been a leader some 550 years before. Apparently Daniel had taught this learned order about the prophetic signs that would indicate the general time of the Messiah's birth. Their appearance accentuated the blindness of Israel's religious leaders to the prophecies concerning the Messiah's first advent as "a humble, suffering servant."

King Herod gathered the chief priests and scribes together and was told that the King-Messiah would be born **"In Bethlehem of Judea, for so it has been written by the prophet"** (v.5).

THE SON OF GOD

A serious exploration of the hundreds of prophecies concerning the Messiah will lead to only one conclusion: only Jesus of Nazareth could have fulfilled them all.

Χριστοζ, or *Christ*, the Greek word for "Messiah" was only one of the names given to Jesus. He was often called "the Son of Man" to express His true humanity and His kinship with the human race whom He came to save. This seems to have been Jesus' favorite name. He was always aware of His eternal deity, but being human was a novelty to Him.

He was called the "the Son of God" because God Himself was the Father of His human nature.

The angel's announcement to Mary concerning the conception of Jesus had profound theological significance. After he announced to Mary that she had been chosen to bear the Messiah, Mary accepted the honor by faith and asked how such a thing would be possible, since she had never known a man. In response, the angel gave this simple, yet profound answer, **"The Holy Spirit will come upon you, and the power of the Most High will overshadow you; and for that reason the *holy offspring* shall be called the Son of God"** (Luke 1:35).

You see, it is only **"the holy offspring"** that is **"the Son of God."** The second person of the Godhead existed from all eternity and created all things that exist. He could not be born. But the human nature who became Jesus of Nazareth is the Son of God for one simple reason — God

Himself *is* His father.

The title "Son of God" could not speak of Christ's deity — His divine nature did not require a father. This is how so many Christians get tripped up by Jehovah Witnesses, Mormons and Muslims who use this issue to prove their point that Jesus could not be equal with God. Most Christians fail to distinguish between the divine and human natures of Jesus. If the entire person of Jesus was born as the Son of God, he couldn't be equal to God because He would have a beginning.

The Roman Catholics miss this point also by calling Mary the "mother of God." The very title is a contradiction — How could the eternal God be born of a mortal woman? The Triune God is the only eternal, self-existent being in the universe according to the Bible. For Mary to be the mother of God would make her greater than God.

During His ministry on earth, Jesus spoke of Himself as being both God and Man. In His deity He is *coequal* with God, but in His humanity, He was *subject* to God, His Father.

Referring to His divine nature, Christ said, **"I and My Father are one"** — literally in the Greek, "one essence" (John 10:30 NKJV). This was an unqualified claim of total equality with God.

But speaking from His human nature (which was His most common point of reference in the Gospels), Jesus declared, **"If you loved Me, you would rejoice because I said, 'I am going to the Father, *for My Father is greater than I*'"** (John 14:28).

THE HYPOSTATIC UNION

This is a big theological term, but it is the name of the church's historical orthodox stand on the person of Jesus Christ.

It means that the Scriptures teach: the Lord Jesus Christ has two natures that are inseparably united — total deity and true humanity. These two natures are united in one person, without confusion or mixture of attributes or function. The union is personal and eternal.

In the Gospels, Jesus would sometimes speak from His human nature, sometimes from His deity and sometimes from a combination of the two natures. The most exciting challenge is to study the Gospels and determine in each situation from which nature Jesus is speaking. The Lord Jesus, the Messiah, is the unique person of the universe. No one else is like Him.

The Lord Jesus is equal to God the Father and God the Holy Spirit, yet different in that He is also man. He is one with man and yet He is different because He is also the Eternal God Almighty. As we will see, this is the reason why He, and He alone, can be the Mediator between God and Man. As it is written, **"For there is one God and one mediator between God and men, the man Christ Jesus..."** (1 Timothy 2:5 NIV).

OUT OF ETERNITY INTO TIME

Jesus Christ who, as God, always existed in the Godhead with the Father and the Holy Spirit, some two thousand years ago left the Throne of God to come to earth and become a man. Considering the repugnance this must have meant for One who had never known anything but the sinlessness of heaven, we should consider carefully why He did it.

Let's enumerate *seven reasons* why God found it necessary to take on visible form and become the man Jesus Christ.

First: God became a man in order to be the Savior of men.

In writing about the origin of Jesus, the Apostle John calls Him a unique name, **"the Word."** He says the Word existed before the beginning of all things. He was there face to face with God and was, in fact, God (John 1:1).

Then John says, **"And the Word became flesh, and dwelt among us, and we beheld His glory, glory as of the only begotten from the Father, full of grace and truth"** (John 1:14).

There's no possible way to misunderstand what John is saying. You may disagree with it, but his statement is clear. This One, called **"the Word,"** who was present in the beginning of time and who was God, took on flesh and dwelt here on earth with men.

Why do you suppose Jesus was called "the Word"? It's because He was the personification of all that the Father wanted to say to men.

TWO CONDITIONS CONTRASTED

On several occasions in the New Testament, Jesus is referred to as "the second Adam." It's because as a man He perfectly fulfilled all the dreams and aspirations that God had originally had for the first Adam.

The two conditions of mankind are often contrasted by what Adam brought down on man and what Jesus did to reverse it. Let's look at several of these contrasts.

"For since by a man [Adam] **came death, by a man** [Jesus] **also came the resurrection of the dead. For as in Adam all die, so also in Christ all shall be made alive"** (1 Corinthians 15:21,22).

"For if by the transgression of the one [Adam], **death reigned through the one, much more those who**

receive the abundance of grace and of the gift of righteousness will reign in life through the One, Jesus Christ.
So then as through one transgression [Adam's] there
resulted condemnation to all men; even so through one act
of righteousness [Christ's death] there resulted justification
of life to all men. For as through the one man's disobedience [Adam's] the many [mankind] were made sinners,
even so through the obedience of the One [Jesus] the many
will be made righteous" (Romans 5:17-19).

The point of all these verses is that the first man got
mankind into all its trouble, but God sent another Man into
the world and He undid it.

In order to qualify as a true human being who could
undo sin's damage, Jesus did not use His divine power while
He was on earth. Paul tells us that "although He existed in
the form of God, [He] did not regard equality with God a
thing to be clung to, but He laid aside His divine privileges, taking the form of a bond-servant, and being made
in the likeness of men" (Philippians 2:6,7 paraphrased).

Jesus' whole life was lived in total dependence upon
the Father who worked through Him by the Holy Spirit who
indwelt Him. That's the exact way that God intended for all
men to live. If Jesus had ever withstood one temptation or
performed one miracle using His own divine power, He
would not have been behaving as a true man and He would
have disqualified Himself from being the Savior of men. (See
John 5:19,30.)

Now, let's look at another reason why God had to
become man.

**Second: God became a man so that He could die for man's
sin.** What is sin's penalty? Death. Can God die? Obviously

not. Therefore the One who would take the penalty for man had to be a mortal human being as well as truly God.

The writer of Hebrews made this clear, **"But we see Jesus, who was made a little lower than the angels...that He, by the grace of God, might taste death for everyone"** (Hebrews 2:9 NKJV).

"And being found in appearance as a man, He [Jesus] **humbled Himself by becoming obedient to the point of death, even death on a cross"** (Philippians 2:8).

Not only could Jesus die for men, but He was willing to do so. It's one thing to have a friend who could give His life for you, but it's quite another thing to find one who actually would!

Jesus was born to die!

We all have death ahead of us as a consequence of our fallen natures. But Jesus knew when He came into the world that His main mission in life was to die for men (Hebrews 10:5-10). What a thing to have hanging over your head all your life! Yet the Bible tells us, it was because of the joy that was set before Him that He endured the shame and pain of the cross (Hebrews 12:2). That joy was the anticipation of removing all the barriers between God and man and bringing about a reconciliation.

Third: God became a man to be a mediator. A mediator is one who effects a reconciliation between estranged parties. Recall what Paul wrote to Timothy, **"For there is one God, and one mediator also between God and men, the man Christ Jesus"** (1 Timothy 2:5).

Back in the Book of Job the "daysman" or "mediator" showed us that in order to be a go-between, it was necessary to be equal to both persons involved in the mediation (Job 9).

The One who could bring man and God back together had to be equal to both.

This qualification narrows it down quickly to only One in the history of the universe — Jesus Christ, the God-man.

This mediator had to be the sinless Son of God in order to have the quality of righteousness acceptable to a holy God in the mediation. Jesus had that kind of personal perfection, and as a confirmation of that fact, when He was being baptized in the River Jordan, a voice out of heaven spoke saying, **"This is My beloved Son, in whom I am well pleased"** (Matthew 3:17).

The mediator also had to be able to sympathize with the predicament of man, and thus he had to also be a true man, but a man who never sinned.

Jesus was this man.

Fourth: God had to become a man to be our priest. A priest is a man who represents humanity's cause before God. He has to experience all the temptations and trials of men in order to be a sympathetic and knowledgeable intercessor for men.

Six chapters in the Book of Hebrews are devoted to a discussion of the priesthood of Jesus (Hebrews 4, 5, 7, 8, 9, 10). But six verses sum up the work of Jesus as mankind's high priest.

"And the former priests [those who lived in Israel's past history], **on the one hand, existed in greater numbers, because they were prevented by death from continuing** [in office], **but He** [Jesus], **on the other hand, because He abides forever, holds His priesthood permanently.**

"Hence also He is able to save forever those who

draw near to God through Him, since He always lives to make intercession for them.

"For it was fitting that we should have such a high priest [as Jesus], holy, innocent, undefiled, separated from sinners and exalted above the heavens; who does not need daily, like those high priests [of old], to offer up sacrifices, first for His own sins, and then for the sins of the people, because this He did once for all when He offered up Himself.

"For the Law appoints men as high priests who are weak, but the word of the oath, which came after the Law, appoints a Son, made perfect forever" (Hebrews 7:23-28).

Jesus is a high priest who's been in our shoes. He knows what it's like to live under the pressures and temptations of this world. **"For we do not have a high priest who cannot sympathize with our weaknesses, but one who has been tempted in all things as we are, yet without sin. Let us therefore draw near with confidence to the throne of grace, that we may receive mercy and may find grace to help in time of need"** (Hebrews 4;15,16).

Fifth: He had to become man to be the revealer of God. Man, in his spiritual death, had lost any accurate concept of God. God had to become visible to us in terms that our soulish life could grasp, and Jesus is God made real in human form.

Jesus said of Himself, **"He who has seen Me has seen the Father..."** and, **"I and the Father are one"** (John 14:9; 10:30). In a very real sense, Jesus is a living photograph of the Father. All that God wanted revealed of Himself,

He revealed in the Person of His Son, Jesus.

But Jesus is not only the revealer of the Father to man, He's also the revealer of the Father's plan to redeem mankind. The Holy Spirit reveals, **"In the past God spoke to our forefathers through the prophets at many times and in various ways, but in these last days he has spoken to us by his Son, whom he appointed heir of all things, and through whom he made the universe. This Son is the radiance** [the blazing forth] **of God's glory and the exact representation of his being, sustaining all things by his powerful word..."** (Hebrews 1:1-3 NIV).

Sixth: God became a man to occupy King David's throne. One of the great prophecies of the coming Messiah was that He would be a direct blood descendant of King David. God spoke this promise to David, **"I will set up your seed after you...and I will establish his throne forever"** (1 Chronicles 17:11,12 NKJV). God's eternal government would be built **"...upon the throne of David"** (Isaiah 9:7).

The importance of this fact cannot be overestimated. This is why the first sixteen verses of the New Testament document the genealogy from David to Christ.

Look closely at what the angel said to Mary about the miraculous conception that would take place in her womb: **"He will be great, and will be called the Son of the Most High; and the Lord God will give Him the throne of His father David; and He will reign over the house of Jacob forever, and His kingdom will have no end"** (Luke 1:32,33).

Through Mary, the Messiah was given the blood right to the throne of David, because she was descended from the line of David's son, Nathan. This was important because a curse was put upon the legal line from Solomon because of the awful sins of his descendant, Jeconiah. (See Jeremiah 22:24-30.) If Jesus had been the actual son of Joseph, who was from Solomon's line, He would have been under the curse of Jeconiah. But by adoption, He got Joseph's legal right to David's throne without the blood curse.

Seventh: God had to become a man in order to be a "kinsman redeemer." This is a concept taught in the Old Testament, especially in the Book of Ruth. In the Law of Moses, whenever a Jewish person was put into slavery, the only one who could pay the ransom price to release him was **"nearest kinsman"** (Leviticus 25:25). This was to establish the principle that whoever would be the one to free mankind from its slavery to Satan would have to be a "near of kin" to the ones being freed, in this case the human race. In taking on humanity, Jesus became a "kinsman" of men and qualified to be the "kinsman redeemer." This is one of the reasons that Jesus loved to call Himself the Son of Man.

JESUS, THE GOD-MAN

In the last two chapters we've examined many lines of evidence that clearly shows why it was necessary for God to come into this world, clothed with a human body. We've also seen that the complete humanity which was prepared for Him to live in while here on earth for thirty-three years was none other than Jesus of Nazareth.

Jesus was fully aware that He was God in the flesh — Incarnate Deity. He boldly declared that:

—He came from God (John 6:38,15; 16:27,28: 17:5).

—He actually *was* God (John 10:30; John 20:26-29; Mark 14:61,62).

—He was to be worshipped (Matthew 8:2,3; 9:18; 14:33).

—He could forgive people of their sins, which only God had the power to do (Mark 2:5-12; Matthew 9:1-8).

—He would rise from the dead (Matthew 27:62-66; Mark 8:31,32; 9:31).

—He would return to the Father to prepare a dwelling place for His children (John 14:1-3).

—He would one day return to earth to take us with Him into heaven (Acts 1:10,11).

Those declarations are too powerful to be ignored. If Jesus said these things about Himself, we are faced with the question He asked the disciples: **"Who do you say that I am?"** (Mark 8:29).

Millions of people will tell you, "I believe Jesus was a great moral teacher, but I don't accept His claim to be God."

WAS HE TELLING THE TRUTH?

So what do you do with a man who said all these things about Himself? You can't dismiss it simply because you don't want to make a judgment as to His truthfulness or sanity. You must come to some conclusion in your own mind about Jesus.

As C. S. Lewis, the brilliant British scholar, said of Jesus in his wonderful book, *Mere Christianity:*

"I'm trying here to prevent anyone saying the really foolish thing that people often say about Jesus: 'I'm ready to accept Jesus as a great moral teacher, but I don't accept His claim to be God.' That is the one thing we must not say. A man who was merely a man and said the sort of things Jesus said would not be a great moral teacher. He would either be a lunatic—on the level with the man who says he is a poached egg—or else he would be the Devil of Hell. You must make your choice. Either this man was, and is, the Son of God, or else a madman or something worse. You can shut Him up for a fool, you can spit at Him and kill Him as a demon, or you can fall at His feet and call Him Lord and God. But let us not come up with any patronizing nonsense about His being just a great human teacher. He has not left that open to us. He did not intend to."[1]

There is only one intellectually honest conclusion after you objectively consider all the facts: *He is the promised Messiah, the Son of the living God.*

One hymn writer put it beautifully:
The Word became flesh
And died as my Savior.
What mercy,
What love,
And what grace.

---

1. C. S. Lewis, *Mere Christianity* (New York: The Macmillan Company, 1943).

CHAPTER 9

PROPITIATION

OR WHY GOD
AIN'T MAD ANYMORE

'Twas grace that taught my heart to fear,
And grace my fears relieved;
How precious did that grace appear,
The hour I first believed.
— JOHN NEWTON

In the last two chapters we've looked at why God had to become a man and why it could have been no other man but Jesus.

Now I want to show why Jesus had to go to the cross — why there was no other way for God to reconcile men to Himself.

WHY A HUMAN SACRIFICE?

But why was it necessary for Christ to die on the cross? The most repugnant aspect of Christianity to a Jew is the idea of human sacrifice. This is what God condemned in the pagan cultures all about them. What was different in the death of Jesus? Was there no other possibility for God to reconcile men to Himself?

The first and the most important reason for Christ's death on the cross is called "propitiation." Don't be scared by this word. It's a beautiful word which means to "turn away wrath by the satisfaction of violated justice." Webster's dictionary defines the word simply as "to appease and render favorable; to conciliate and reconcile." The biblical definintion is much more carefully developed than that.

Christ's act of propitiation was to remove the barrier of God's offended attributes of righteousness and justice. This was by far the most difficult of all the barriers to a relationship with God.

When Jesus hung on the cross, He bore the compounded fury of God's just wrath against the sins of the entire human race. Now God has no more wrath to pour out on men. His justice is satisfied because a perfectly righteous man volunteered to take the wrath of offended righteousness and justice in place of all men. This act of propitiation removed God's wrath. As one southern brother put it, "God ain't mad anymore. He took all His anger out on Jesus."

IS IT RIGHT FOR GOD TO HAVE WRATH?

It's amazing to me that there are so many theologians around who are saying, "Oh, if you teach propitiation as a removal of God's wrath, you're contributing to the idea of a petty God who simply has to be appeased in order to be happy."

So, because they only want to think about a God of love, they try to do away with the fact that the Bible deals in depth with the truth of God's just wrath against sin. In the Old Testament alone, God's wrath against sin is mentioned 585 times.[1]

God's wrath is also a very important reality in the New Testament, but there the emphasis is on the propitiation of Christ, which has removed God's wrath from mankind. (See John 3:36; Romans 9:22; Ephesians 5:6; Colossians 3:6.)

GOD CAN'T RULE BY "THE WARM FUZZIES"

Because we are human we don't always look at everything in terms of black and white. We let our sympathy blur our judgment at times.

But God, as the sovereign and righteous Judge of the

universe, must direct His wrath against sin, wherever it's found and in whomever it's found. He can't let His love for man cause Him to compromise His just condemnation of man's sin.

For instance, I know a judge who is a very warm and loving person with real empathy for human needs. He has certainly overlooked and dismissed wrongs done to him in the sphere of his family and friends. But when he is officially in the role of a judge, even though a member of his family has broken the law, he can't sweep the facts under the table and not execute the penalty. If he did, he'd no longer be qualified to judge. A judge who shows partiality and inequity in the administration of the law is unacceptable in any society.

How much more so in the case of God. He's not only our Creator, but also the Judge of the universe. As such, He doesn't have the liberty of breaking the very laws which inherently emanate from His character. If He did, the universe would be in chaos. There would be no absolute standards at all that anyone could count on.

No! God's wrath is real, but so is His solution— Christ's propitiatory death on the cross.

PROPITIATION PROPOUNDED

Since this concept of propitiation is so new to many, let's look at it more in depth. The central passage in the New Testament that teaches the doctrine of propitiation is Romans 3:25,26.

There are two important points I want to emphasize about propitiation. First, when the Bible says Christ died to satisfy the offended righteousness and justice of God, and to turn away wrath from those who believe in Him, this even included believers in the Old Testament who lived before the cross! That's what it means when it says in that passage, **"He passed over the sins previously committed."** God put the sins of those Old Testament saints on a charge account which was guaranteed to be paid by the promise of a coming Savior. (See Isaiah 53; Jeremiah 31:31-34.)

But the second emphasis of this passage in Romans 3 is that Jesus was displayed **"publicly"** as a propitiation. God did this so that the whole world would know that His offended character had been "satisfied" by Jesus' death and that now He remained perfectly just in declaring righteous all who would believe in His Son's substitutionary death on their behalf.

THE TENT IN THE WILDERNESS

Perhaps the clearest example in the Bible of what propitiation means is found in its Old Testament counterpart. The Greek word for "propitiation" is *hilasterion* (ιλαστεριον). This is the same word for the Old Testament Hebrew word for "mercy seat."

The "mercy seat" was part of the furniture God told Moses to build and set in a special place of worship in the wilderness. This special worship building was a portable tent-like affair which served the Hebrews in their worship of their God while they traveled in the Sinai Wilderness for forty years. It was called the "Tabernacle."

This was the place where God came down to meet with men through the intercession of their high priest, and it was the place where men came to meet God and have their sins forgiven through the system of animal sacrifices which God had instructed Moses to institute.

Everything about this Tabernacle and its articles of furniture was intended to portray in a temporary way what God would one day do permanently. The animal sacrifices foreshadowed the many facets of what God would do one day when He provided "the Lamb" of His choosing.

That "Lamb" was His Son, Jesus. Recall what John the Baptist said of Jesus when He saw Him coming toward him, **"Behold, the Lamb of God who takes away the sin of the world!"** (John 1:29).

LEVI & SONS' FURNITURE, LTD.

There were a number of pieces of important furniture in the two rooms in the Tabernacle which the priestly tribe of Levi used in their daily intercessions for the people.

But the most important article in the entire Tabernacle was located in the inner room called the "Holy of Holies." This was the room where God's presence dwelt on earth, and it was the place of "propitiation" for God. The central object in the room was a rather small acacia wood box, covered with gold. God had given Moses exact instructions on how to make this "Ark of the Covenant." You can learn the details of its construction in Exodus 25.

Everything about this focal piece of furniture was symbolic of the Person and work of God's coming Lamb, Jesus Christ. The wood represented His humanity, the gold His deity. The top, or lid, of this ark was solid gold. The throne on top became known as the "mercy seat," which the original New Testament word *hilasterion* describes as "the place of propitiation."

God left nothing to chance in His detailed blueprint to Moses as to how this Ark of the Covenant was to be con-

structed. Each tiny part of it held awesome symbolic meaning in God's eternal plan to redeem fallen mankind.

Extremely significant were the gold figures of two
angels called "cherubim," made facing each other with out-
stretched wings, looking down upon the mercy seat. (The
"im" suffix was the Hebrew equivalent of an "s" to make the
word plural.) Cherubs were an order of angels always associ-
ated with guarding the Holiness of God.

Underneath this mercy seat, where God instructed the
face of the angels to be looking, were three peculiar items
described for us in Hebrews 9:1-6.

MANNA FOR ALL SEASONS

First, God told Moses to place inside the ark a pot of
manna. You'll remember that manna was a food God provided for the Israelites during their forty-year tour of the Sinai
wilderness. At first the people had welcomed this miraculous
provision, but soon they began griping about it and asked for
more variety in their diet.

"We wish we had some of those delicious foods — the
leeks, the garlics — we had back in Egypt," they murmured.

Their attitude really grieved God. After all, no one
had gotten sick in those forty years, so manna must have been
a perfect food.

So God said, "Put the manna in the pot and put it in
the ark." This became a symbol of man's rejection of God's
material provisions.

A ROD TO REMEMBER

The second item for the Ark originated from a rebellion within the camp of Israel against Moses' and Aaron's

leadership (Numbers 16,17). After God had dealt with the rebel instigators, He called the tribal leaders to come before Moses. The symbol of leadership was a rod, or wooden staff. Moses took a rod from each one of the rebel leaders and deposited all twelve in the Tabernacle overnight. The man whose rod sprouted leaves was the one God wanted as the leader.

When the rods were taken from the Tabernacle the next day, Aaron's had sprouted leaves. But the Israelites disobeyed Aaron's and Moses' leadership anyway. His rod was placed inside the ark as a reminder of man's rejection of God's leadership.

STONES THAT SPEAK

The third item in the ark was the stones upon which the Ten Commandments were inscribed. After Moses had received the two tablets of the Law written by the finger of God, he came down the mountain, only to find the people in rebellion and idolatry. The gross sins of the crowd angered Moses so much, he flung the tablets onto the ground and they broke in pieces. God had the boken pieces placed inside the ark as a witness that man broke His Law.

The ark, therefore, contained the physical representations of man's total sinfulness—

—the manna: man's rejection of God's *provision*

— Aaron's rod: man's rejection of God's *leadership*

—the broken tablets of the law: man's rejection of God's *holiness*.

THE DAY OF ATONEMENT

The Ark of the Covenant was located in the Holy of Holies, the inner chamber of the Tabernacle. Only one man

in all the world was allowed in that chamber, the high priest
of Israel — and he, only once a year on the Day of Atonement
(Yom Kippor). On that day he would take the blood of an
animal sacrifice and sprinkle it over the top of the mercy seat.

As mentioned above, cherubs in the Bible are associ-
ated with the holiness of God, as His guardians and servants
in His presence (Ezekiel 1; Genesis 3:24). It appears that one
of the cherubs hovering over the mercy seat represented the
absolute righteousness of God; the other, His perfect justice.

When the cherub of righteousness looked down on
the symbols in the Ark, he saw the three evidences of man's
sin. The cherub of justice looked down and saw the evidence
that man was no longer acceptable to God's righteousness and
pronounced the penalty of death upon man.

HOW WRATH BECOMES MERCY

But on the Day of Atonement, what did the angels
see? The symbols of sin?

No. They saw the blood of a divinely ordained innocent sacrifice covering the symbols of sin. Justice could now
say, "I'm satisfied or propitiated, because the death penalty
has been paid." Righteousness said, "I'm no longer offended
because the evidence of man's sin has been covered from my
eyes and I see only the blood of an innocent substitute who
paid the required penalty of death."

One more thing is very important here symbolically.
The golden lid, or mercy seat, was comparable to being God's
throne on earth, because He said He dwelt between the cherubim.

**"And there I will meet with you, and from above
the mercy seat, from between the two cherubim which are**

upon the ark of the testimony, I will speak to you..."
(Exodus 25:22).

Until the blood of the animal was sprinkled on the mercy seat, this throne of God depicted a place of judgment. But, covered by the blood once a year, it became a throne of mercy, or mercy seat. God could now sit upon this throne and show the facet of His character called "mercy" because His righteousness and justice were completely satisfied by the blood sacrifice which He had ordained! Once His righteousness and justice were satisfied, God could pour out His love on a just basis to anyone who came by faith alone, recognizing he had no merit acceptable to God. His love poured out on the basis of propitiation is what we call GRACE.

"I will appear in the cloud over the mercy seat," God said in Leviticus 16:2. Here was the place where estranged man could now meet God through the mediation of the sacrifice.

The symbolism represented in the sacrificial system and the worship in the Tabernacle is really beautiful. Through this picture the Old Testament believers could learn about the nature of God and His Messiah, and how God would one day provide a perfect final sacrifice.

A SHADOW OF THINGS TO COME

I've gone into some detail about the Tabernacle, and particularly the Ark of the Covenant, because it's written about them that they are **"a copy and shadow of the heavenly things."** In fact, that's why Moses was warned by God when he was about to build the Tabernacle *that he should make everything about it exactly according to the pattern God showed him while He was up on Mount Sinai.* It was to be a copy and picture of things which actually exist in heaven (Hebrews 8:5).

This command of God takes on great importance when we start analyzing the various functions of the Tabernacle and attempting to see the deeper truths that they were "foreshadowing." We have to keep in mind that whatever was enacted in symbol and type in the earthly tabernacle where God dwelt, was either being enacted, or would be in the future, in the heavenly tabernacle where God dwells now.

JESUS IS THE REAL THING

I usually go into detail and spend months teaching the lessons of the Tabernacle when I teach Old Testament classes. I spend so much time because every function and symbol of the tabernacle worship found its deeper fulfillment in the life, death, and resurrection of Jesus Christ. Only God could have so perfectly planned such a detailed and minute correlation between the "shadow" and its ultimate reality.

If you want a fascinating and rewarding study of all the ways in which Jesus fulfilled the types pictured in the Tabernacle, I suggest you read Dr. J. Vernon McGee's book, *Tabernacle, God's Portrait of Christ.*[2]

I also suggest a thorough reading of the Book of Hebrews, since it's in this book that much of this typology is unraveled for us.

The New Testament writer of the Book of Hebrews had as his main audience the thousands of Hebrews who had accepted Jesus as the promised Messiah. The writer must have been Jewish, since he had such a perfect understanding of the correlation of the Old Testament symbols of worship and Christ's fulfillment of them.

THE ONLY PERFECT HIGH PRIEST

Because our particular interest in this chapter deals with Christ's propitiatory work for man, I want to center on His role as high priest.

In the tabernacle worship, it was the role of the high priest to enter the Holy of Holies once a year and place the blood of an innocent sacrifice onto the mercy seat and thereby obtain God's mercy for the people for another year.

Listen to what the writer of Hebrews says of Jesus: **"But when Christ appeared as a high priest of the good things to come, He entered through the greater and more perfect tabernacle, not made with hands, that is to say, not of this creation; and not through the blood of goats and calves, but through His own blood, He entered the holy place once for all, having obtained eternal redemption"** (Hebrews 9:11,12).

This statement overflows with beautiful analogy! Jesus, as our high priest, actually entered the Holy of Holies in heaven with the blood of an perfect sacrifice — HIS OWN BLOOD. There He sprinkled it on the mercy seat of the heavenly tabernacle and obtained, not just a temporary, year-long forgiveness for men, but an *eternal* redemption.

Note it says He did it **"once for all,"** and by this **"He obtained eternal redemption."** How long is "eternal?" This means it never has to be done again and again as the former priests had to do, *because it redeems those who receive it for eternity.* All those saved by this sacrifice are saved forever — they can *never* be lost again.

THINK OF IT!

This one act of Jesus, Who is both the High Priest and the perfect sacrifice, has forever *satisfied* or *propitiated* God's justice and righteousness. His infinitely efficacious blood has been put on record at the throne of God so that it will forever remind the Father that His wrath has already been fully poured out upon the sin of all men. As the Holy Spirit revealed, **"My little children, these things I write to you, that you may not sin. And if anyone sins, we have an Advocate with the Father, Jesus Christ the righteous. And He Himself is the propitiation for our sins, and not for ours only but also for the whole world"** (1 John 2:1-2 NKJV).

The blood of Jesus is our guarantee that God will never again be angry with anyone who believes in Jesus as his personal Savior. Jesus' blood has turned God's throne from one of judgment to one of mercy.

The substitutionary death of Christ has removed the barrier of God's offended character for all men — the whole world. God's wrath has been conciliated, and He is now free to deal with every man individually on the basis of grace.

THE *ONE SIN* FOR WHICH CHRIST COULD NOT DIE

There are some who believe that since Christ took man's sin to the cross, the Father will never again show His righteous anger. That is not the case. Scripture makes it clear that **"He who believes in the Son has everlasting life; and he who does not believe the Son shall not see life, but *the wrath of God abides on him*"** (John 3:36 NKJV).

But what has changed is the reason for the wrath. It is not because of the unbeliever's *sins*, they have been paid for. It is because of the one great sin of rejecting Christ's propitiatory sacrifice on his behalf. This is why the Holy Spirit now convicts the unbeliever of the one unpardonable sin, **"And He** [the Holy Spirit]**, when He comes, will convict the world concerning sin, and righteousness, and judgment; concerning sin,** *because they do not believe in Me...*" (John 16:8-9).

Rejecting the pardon Jesus died to make free to you is the one sin for which He could not die.

---

1. For a good Bible study tool both in this area and in general, let me recommend *Young's Analytical Concordance.* If you look up the word "wrath" in this volume, for example, it will show you every place it is used in the Bible and how it is used. It will categorize the English translation with the word in the original language it was written in.

2. J. Vernon McGee, *Tabernacle, God's Portrait of Christ* (Thru the Bible Books).

CHAPTER 10

REDEMPTION

NO LONGER SLAVES

In the last chapter we saw the first barrier between God and man, GOD'S HOLY CHARACTER, being torn down by the propitiation of Christ. That was the work of Christ in presenting His blood upon the mercy seat in heaven and obtaining permanent forgiveness for men by satisfying the outraged holiness of God.

Redemption is the work of Jesus Christ on our behalf to cancel out our DEBT OF SIN and release us from SLAVERY TO SATAN and the SIN NATURE. These two terrible barriers were torn down by the redemptive work of Christ on the cross.

OUR CERTIFICATE OF DEBT

In chapter four, when we were discussing how man had incurred his DEBT OF SIN, we saw that the Apostle Paul, in describing this indebtedness, had used a scene right out of the Roman law courts.

Every time a Roman citizen was convicted of a crime, the jurisprudence of the day demanded that a "Certificate of Debt" be prepared. On this certificate the criminal's unlawful deeds were listed, one by one, and the exact penalty he owed. He would be sent to jail and the Certificate of Debt was nailed on the outside of his cell door. And it hung there until the man had served his time and thereby paid the penalty for those crimes listed on the certificate.

Listen to the powerful way Paul convinces his hearers that they have been set free from their sinful indebtedness to God, **"And when you were dead in your transgressions and the uncircumcision of your flesh, He made you alive together with Him, having forgiven us all our transgressions, having canceled out the certificate of debt consisting of decrees against us and which was hostile to us; and He has taken it out of the way, having nailed it to the cross"** (Colossians 2:13,14).

Our Certificate of Debt consists of decrees — God's laws which we've broken — and they stand against us. God's decrees are "hostile" to us because we cannot keep them, without breaking some of them. There's nothing wrong with God's laws; they're perfect. The problem is our complete inability to keep them.

Paul gives us a fantastic picture here of Jesus taking our Certificate of Debt and nailing it to His cross. In doing this, it was tantamount to saying He made Himself guilty for every sin listed on every human being's certificate of debt. Not only did He volunteer to take our certificates, but also our penalty of death the certificates demanded.

THE DAY THE PLANET WAS LIBERATED

Let's take a brief glance at that day in history that forever altered the relationship of God and man — the day Jesus died.

Here's how it happened. Jesus was nailed to the cross at about 9:00 in the morning. He prayed for those who had nailed Him there. Then He made provision for His mother, turning her over to the keeping of His disciple, John. Just before noon He began His dialog with the two criminals on each side of Him, and one of them turned in repentance to Him as his Lord and Savior. This believing murderer was promised a place in paradise, beginning at the moment of his death.

At noonday God drew a veil of darkness over the whole earth. It was pitch black. I believe God did this so that no one would be able to witness visually the horror of what was happening to Jesus as He hung there— because in that moment, all the wrath of God was engulfing Him as He allowed the sins of all mankind to be put on Him.

Until then Jesus hadn't uttered even a whimper.

THE FINAL YOM KIPPOR

But then, all of a sudden, the silence was broken and Jesus cried out from His human nature, **"Eloi, Eloi, lama sabachthani, which is translated 'My God, My God, why have You forsaken Me?'"** (Mark 15:34 KNJV).

In that instant God had taken the Certificates of Debt of every human being from the beginning of mankind until the close of history, and nailed them to the cross, making Jesus responsible and guilty for each one!

Even God had to turn His back on His own Son in His greatest hour of need, because Jesus, His only Son, had voluntarily allowed Himself to be made guilty for the sin of the whole world. Because God is Holy, He cannot have fellowship with sin of any kind — and Jesus was now made sin on our behalf. How heart-wrenching it is to realize even a little of what our redemption cost the Father, the Son and the Holy Spirit.

When I get to heaven I want to ask Jesus, "Lord, what

really happened in that awful period of blackness?"

Even after He explains it to me, I know I won't be able to comprehend what it really was like for the poured-out fury of a holy God to fall like an atomic blast on Jesus.

THE MYSTERY OF ALL MYSTERIES

His scream was out of deep agony of soul because, for the first and last time for all eternity, the Second Person of the Godhead, Jesus, was separated from the other two members of the Godhead, the Father and the Spirit.

No one will ever be as alone as Jesus was on the cross. He was separated from every person He'd ever loved and trusted. Forsaken by His closest friends, forsaken by God the Father and God the Holy Spirit, forsaken by all, He hung there in an aloneness that nobody will ever be able to fathom.

I'm convinced this is why Jesus screamed "My God, My God" — twice. He was addressing "My God, the Father" and "My God, the Holy Spirit." God, the Son was hanging on a Roman cross, bound to His humanity that was bearing the sin of the world.

DO YOU KNOW WHY HE DID IT?

So that you and I would never have to be alone again. So that He can now promise those who believe in Him, "I will never desert you, nor will I ever forsake you" (Hebrews 13:5).

THE CRY THAT SHOOK THE WORLD

But that's not the end of the story.

Just before Jesus gave up His earthly life and commended His Spirit to the Father, He shouted a word which is the Magna Carta of freedom for all true believers.

That victorious cry was the Greek word, *tetelestai* (τετελεσται) (John 19:30).

Let that word burn like a firebrand into your mind, because that's the exact same word that a Roman judge would write across a released criminal's Certificate of Debt to show that all his penalty had been paid and he was free at last. The word used in this way means "paid in full." It is translated in John 19:30 as "It is finished," but should be "Paid in Full."

In the mind of God, "Paid in Full" has been written with the blood of Jesus Christ across the Certificate of Debt of every man who will ever live. This certifies forever that our debt to God for sin, slavery to Satan and the sin nature has been fully paid by Jesus. We can never be condemned for all these things again.

But if a man would be so foolish as to insist on staying imprisoned by his sins, even though his debt has been paid, then the Certificate of Debt assuring his freedom is of no benefit to him. And when he comes to the end of his life, he will have to pay the penalty of death and separation from God himself, because of one sin — the sin of rejecting God's free gift of pardon which is reserved in heaven with his name on it.

THE OTHER SIDE OF REDEMPTION

Having our DEBT OF SIN canceled is the first benefit of Christ's redemptive work on the cross. But equal to that is the fact that it also released us from SLAVERY TO SATAN and the power of the indwelling SIN NATURE.

The word "redemption" was a very familiar word in the first century since nearly half the world was involved in slavery in one way or another. The sweetest word a slave could hope to hear was the word "redemption."

Since one of the <u>major barriers</u> between <u>God and man</u> is our <u>SLAVERY TO SATAN,</u> the New Testament writers have freely used the concept of redemption to describe the work of Christ on the cross which has ransomed man from Satan's clutches.

In the Greek language there are several different words for "redemption" which emphasize different aspects of it. Unfortunately, these have all been translated into our one English word "redemption." In order to appreciate the rich meaning of these words, and to fully understand the scope of freedom from SLAVERY TO SATAN which Christ has purchased for us, let's look at four different emphases of the word "redemption."

ΛΥΤΡΟΩ
EMPHASIS ON FREEDOM

The first word is a verb, *lutroo* (λυτροω). Its root meaning is "to set free," and its inherent emphasis is the *state of being free*. Since the word means to be set free from slavery by the payment of a ransom, it's translated "redemption."

The word *lutroo* is used in 1 Peter 1:18,19 as follows: **"Knowing that you were not *redeemed* with perishable things like silver or gold from your futile way of life inherited from your forefathers, but with precious blood, as of a lamb unblemished and spotless, the blood of Christ."**

ΠΕΡΙΠΟΙΕΩ
EMPHASIS ON BEING GOD'S POSSESSION

Another verb is *peripoieo* (περιποιεω), which means "redeemed" but is translated "purchased" in Acts 20:28:

"...shepherd the church of God which He [Jesus] **purchased** [literally: "gained possession of"] **with His own
blood.**" Here the emphasis is not on freedom as such, but on
the means to freedom: the act of buying or gaining possession of something so that it becomes yours to own. Thus,
through redemption we've become God's personal property.

ΑΓΟΡΑΖΩ
EMPHASIS ON THE PLACE OF SLAVERY

A third word is *agorazo* (αγοραζω), coming from the
root noun, *agora* (αγορα), meaning the actual slave market
itself. This derived word came to mean "being set free from
the slave market by paying a ransom." It emphasizes the
awfulness of the place from which we're purchased and is
used in Revelation 5:9: **"Worthy art Thou [Jesus] ...for
Thou wast slain, and did purchase for God with Thy blood
men from every tribe and tongue and people and nation."**

ΕΞΑΓΟΡΑΖΩ
EMPHASIS ON PERMANENCE OF FREEDOM

Then there's a final verb, which is the intensive form
of *agorazo*; it's *exagorazo* (εξαγοραζω). The prefix *ex* or *ek*
(εξ) is added which means "out of" ("ex" as in "exit") and
emphasizes *being purchased out of the slave market, never to
be sold as a slave again.*

The implication here is obvious, as the word is used
in Galatians 3:13: **"Christ redeemed us from the curse of
the Law, having become a curse for us..."** The Law is a
"curse" to us because we can't keep it, and that has brought
us under SLAVERY TO SATAN and to sin. But Jesus
redeemed us from this curse, having taken the curse of sin

and death for us. Yet in His resurrection, He once and for all defeated Satan and threw off his temporary dominion over His humanity.

THIS LITTLE "SLAVE" WENT TO MARKET

The Word of God graphically pictures mankind as being not only sinful, but also, as a result, in SLAVERY TO SATAN in a slave market of sin. The Scriptures are very clear that there's only one way out of the dilemma. A redeemer, who is not himself in the slave market, must redeem all mankind out of it.

That redeemer is Jesus. Here's the picture.

SITUATION	INTERPRETATION	REFERENCE
The Slave Market	The World System	1 John 5:19
The Slave Master	Satan	John 12:31
The Slaves	Humanity	Ephesians 2:2, 3
The Problem	Sin	Colossians 2:14
The Highest Bidder	Jesus (Redeemer)	Hebrews 2:14,15
The Ransom Price	Blood of Christ	1 Peter 1:18,19

Jesus said, **"Every one who commits sin is the slave of sin"** (John 8:34). Since everyone commits sin (if you ever run into somebody who says he doesn't, check with his friends), we are all slaves. It's a condition we are born into with Satan as the father and head of the fallen race of mankind (John 8:44). He energizes the unbelievers

(Ephesians 2:14), and He has power over the whole world system as well (1 John 5:19).

Have you ever wondered why the world's in the mess it's in? Consider the source!

The evil in the world is not just some impersonal force. We're dealing with the reality of a personal being so influential that the whole world has fallen prey to his devices. **"For our struggle is not against flesh and blood, but against the rulers, against the powers, against the world-forces of this darkness, against the spiritual forces of wickedness in the heavenly places"** (Ephesians 6:12).[1]

JESUS, THE LIBERATOR!

Into this insane "slave market of sin," God sent His Redeemer to **"...open [men's] eyes so that they may turn from darkness to light and from the dominion of Satan to God"** (Acts 26:18). But Jesus didn't just "happen along"; it was by careful design in the plan of God. God couldn't select just anyone to be the liberator of mankind; he had to meet the qualifications of a redeemer.

And Jesus perfectly did!

In the Roman system of slavery, every citizen of the empire knew that a slave couldn't free himself, nor could he be freed by another slave. It took a free man who was able and willing to pay his ransom to do it.

In the same way, no human being can free another because we're all in the slave market together. The services of a qualified outsider — One chosen by God — are required, as we discussed in chapters seven and eight.

Let's briefly review the qualifications of Jesus as the redeemer of mankind.

SINLESS REDEEMER

First, the one who would redeem men from Satan's slavery had to be without sin himself. After warning His listeners of their slavery to sin, Jesus says, **"The slave does not remain in the house forever;** *the son does remain forever"* (John 8:35).

In other words, the son is a permanent part of the household, the slave is not. And since the son is above the slave, he has authority over the slave and could even set him free if he chose to.

And then Jesus uses an ingenius combination of metaphors. He says, in the very next verse, **"If therefore the Son shall make you free, you shall be free indeed."** In saying this to them, He is equating them with being slaves and is, in essence, telling them that He is the Son of God and He alone has been born free of sin and has the power to set them free from slavery to sin. This meaning was not lost on these proud religious zealots who thought they were already in the family of God. To say this upset them is to use the understatement of the century. They became livid with rage. Jesus demonstrated He was utterly fearless here.

As we've seen already, Jesus is the only man since Adam to be born on this earth free of sin. This is because of His unique conception. God was the father of His humanity, and Jesus' mother was a virgin. Since the culpability for sin is passed from human father to child, Jesus bypassed inherited sin because He had no human father. Jesus remained free because He lived a life that was completely sinless.

It was to this group, of all people, that Jesus flung down His gauntlet and said, **"Can any of you prove me guilty of sin? If I am telling the truth, why don't you believe me?"** (John 8:46 NIV). No one stepped forward to pick up the challenge, even though they hated Him and would have loved to pin some sin on Him.

Thus Jesus met the first qualification for being a redeemer. He Himself was a free man and the only one capable of paying the ransom price.

KINSMAN REDEEMER

Second, the redeemer had to be "near of kinsman" to the human race. Hebrews 2:14,15 explains why this was so: **"Since then the children** [mankind] **share in flesh and blood, He Himself likewise also partook of the same** [flesh and blood], **that through death He might render powerless him who had the power of death, that is, the devil; and might deliver those who through fear of death were subject to slavery all their lives."**

The price of redemption for man has always been the shed blood of an innocent substitute, as we have seen: **"Without shedding of blood, there is no remission** [of sin]" (Hebrews 9:22 NKJV). We also saw the blood of animals could never take the sin away; it only atoned for, or covered, it temporarily until God provided a complete remission of sins through His ultimate sacrifice of Jesus (Hebrews 10:14).

But, since the redemption price had to be the shed blood of an innocent sacrifice, the Redeemer had to be true flesh and blood so that He could actually experience death. In other words, a man, but one who was completely innocent of any sins.

This is why we read concerning Christ's death, **"For you know that it was not with perishable things such as silver or gold that you were redeemed from the empty way of life handed down to you from your forefathers, but with the precious blood of Christ, a lamb without blemish or defect"** (1 Peter 1:18-19 NIV).

MEDIATING REDEEMER

Third, the redeemer had to be a mediator, one who was equal to both parties in the mediation—those in the slave market, and the One seeking to release the slaves. In other words, the redeemer needed to be both God and man. **"For there is one God, and one mediator also between God and men, the man Christ Jesus, who gave Himself as a ransom for all"** (1 Timothy 2:5-6).

WILLING REDEEMER

Finally, in order for a person to become a redeemer, he must do so voluntarily. Certainly a slave was in no position to order a free man to liberate him. The free man would have to be motivated somehow to come and pay the ransom.

When speaking of the life He was to give as a sacrifice for sin, Jesus told the Pharisees in John 10:17,18, **"I lay down My life that I may take it again. No one has taken it away from Me, but I lay it down on My own initiative."**

The reason why?

His love for you and me!

This love is what sent the Lord Jesus to the cross, canceling our DEBT OF SIN and purchasing us out of SLAVERY TO SATAN. These are no longer barriers between God and man — unless we let them be!

FROM JESUS, WITH LOVE!

The redemption that Jesus made available to men at the cross is a love gift. We're not used to receiving things without someone wanting something in return, so it's hard to really grasp the nature of this fantastic offer of a free salvation. In the back of many peoples' minds is the thought that there must be a hidden gimmick somewhere. No one gives something for nothing!

But let me assure you, there's no fine print in the contract of salvation. It doesn't even say that we have to give Him ourselves. All we are asked to do is to take the pardon He's graciously offered us and then begin to enjoy the freedom of a new heart that will always want to follow God. As Paul wrote, **"But now having been freed from sin and enslaved to God, you derive your benefit, resulting in sanctification, and the outcome, eternal life"** (Romans 6:22).

Jesus said, **"Come to Me all you who are weary and heavy laden, and I will give you rest"** (Matthew 11:28). All we have to do is come to Him, give Him our burdens, and take the gift of rest from Him.

John wrote, **"But as many as received Him, to them He gave the right to become children of God, even to those who believe in His name"** (John 1:12). Here again we're asked only to believe in what Jesus did for us in providing our liberation at the cross, and then God gives us the power to become His children.

THE TRAGEDY OF THE "MIGHT-HAVE-BEEN"

As much as I hate to, I must add this final note to this chapter on redemption. Although Christ has redeemed all mankind from Satan's slave market of sin, unfortunately not everyone has chosen to accept the ransom and go free.

The story is told of a young man who was convicted of murder in an eastern state many years ago. His parents, being influential and wealthy, finally obtained a stay of execution from the governor, and eventually the convict was granted a pardon.

This man, still sitting on death row, was given the news that he had been given his freedom. But when he was handed the pardon, he rejected it. He said, "I'm guilty and I want to die."

Try as they could, his family and lawyers couldn't persuade him to change his mind. In an effort to keep him from being executed, the family took the case all the way to the highest court in the state. And the court ruled that a pardon is not a pardon until it is accepted by the one for whom it was intended.

So the man went to his death, not because he had no alternative, but because he refused to accept the pardon.

So it is with men. Those who spend eternity separated from God in bitter anguish of soul and body will do so, not because there isn't an alternative, but because they won't accept the pardon that already has their name on it.

But once a man accepts the pardon, he's forever free. And not just after he dies, either. He's free in this life, in the here-and-now as well as the sweet-by-and-by.

If you've never done so before, why not take this moment to thank Jesus Christ for dying for you, personally, and accept His gracious pardon and forgiveness. You'll be eternally glad you did!

---

1. See author's book, *Satan Is Alive and Well on Planet Earth*, for more details (Zondervan Publishing House, 1972).

CHAPTER 11

SUBSTITUTIONARY DEATH

B illy Graham, in an address at Yale University, told the story of how he was driving through a small town in the South one evening and was picked up by radar in a speed trap. He was clocked at several miles an hour over the speed limit.

A squad car pulled him over and instructed him to follow the car to the local justice of the peace. The justice happened to be a barber, and the office was right there in the barber shop.

Graham tells how he walked into the place and the justice was busy shaving a man. He took his time and finished the job. Then he turned to Graham and quickly reviewed his case. "How do you plead?" the justice asked.

"Guilty, your honor," Graham said.

"That'll be $15," replied the justice.

Graham reached for his wallet to pay the fine.

The justice shot him a second glance and said, "Say, aren't you Billy Graham, the evangelist?"

"I regret to say, sir, that I am," Graham responded, hopefully tucking the wallet back into his pocket.

"That'll be $15," the man said again with a smile.

"But I'll tell you what I'm going to do," said the justice after a moment's hesitation. "I'm going to pay the fine for you."

He reached into his back pocket for his billfold, took it out, removed a five- and a ten-dollar bill, slipped them underneath the cash box in the till, and closed the drawer.

"You've been a big help to me and my family, and this is something I want to do," he said.

JUSTICE ISN'T BLIND

The law had been broken, the penalty assessed, and the fine *had* to be paid.

But in this case, as in the case of God versus mankind, a substitute came forward and volunteered to pay the fine. It didn't cost Billy Graham's "savior" much to pay Billy's fine, but the cost to God to provide a savior to pay our "fine" of death, was the death of His Son.

Substitutionary death is the subject of this chapter. This is the work of Christ on the cross that removed forever the barrier of SPIRITUAL DEATH. Every human being has been born physically alive, but spiritually dead. God can only have a relationship with someone who has His kind of life. So this is that aspect of Christ's death that not only removed our death penalty, but made it possible for God to *restore* His life to every man who believes in His Son.

Just to review briefly:

—*Propitiation* is toward *God*, satisfying His absolute righteousness and justice. Christ's death did that for us.

—*Redemption* is toward *sin*, providing payment of the sin-debt through Jesus' blood. As a result, man has also been set free from the slave market of sin and brought out from under Satan's authority. Christ's death did that for us.

—*Substitutionary Death* is toward our state of *death* here and penalty of death which will separate us from God forever.

Through Christ's substitutionary death for us, both of these terrible barriers are removed.

SIN'S INESCAPABLE PENALTY

The penalty for sin has always been death. One of the first principles Adam and Eve ever learned from God was that *in* the day they ate from the forbidden tree, they would die (Genesis 2:17). They didn't fully understand that "death" meant a spiritual separation from God.

Their first experience with death had been the day the Lord God had killed an innocent animal to obtain its skin to cover their sense of shame and guilt. Then on that sad day when Adam and Eve stood over the lifeless body of their dead son, Abel, they were all too aware of what it meant to die physically.

The final aspect of death is still future and is called "the second death" or eternal death. This will be the final eternal state of all who die on this earth without having their spiritual lives restored. This is *not* a state of eternal unconsciousness, but rather one of very real torment and remorse for ever and ever (Revelation 20:14,15; Matthew 8:12; Luke 16:19-31).

Here is an important maxim to remember:

The one who is born once shall die twice;

But the one who is born twice shall die but once.

THE CONCEPT OF SACRIFICE

In each layer of civilization the archaeologist's spade has uncovered, there has been evidences of sacrifices made to various gods. Since many of these scholars have *not* been prone to accept the bibilical concept of divine creation and the subsequent fall of man, they've used the presence of these numerous artifacts of sacrifice to ridicule and discredit the biblical requirement of substitutionary sacrifice to atone for sin.

They would claim that the Hebrews were only one race out of many who evolved a system of sacrifice to appease an angry god they couldn't fathom. And they would point to sacrificial evidence that predated the appearance of the Hebrew race in their effort to disprove any merit in the biblical concept of animal sacrifice for sins.

But how you interpret the relics of the archaeologist's shovel is entirely dependent on the basic presuppositions you already have about the origin of things. If you believe that man is in a process of evolution from a one-celled organism to some glorious superhuman creature of the future, then you would tend to discount the biblical claim of the fall of man and a subsequent *downward* devolution or degeneration.

But if you accept the biblical claim that God created man full grown, in His own image, and that man distorted that image in himself by rebelling against God, thereby incurring a penalty of death, then you'll see that the concept of substitutionary sacrifice was a necessary *immediate* intervention of God to re-establish a relationship with man.

It would be understandable also as to why every stage of human history has its record of animal and human sacrifices. It's because there was an original true prototype at the beginning of human history from which all the other patterns developed, some staying close to the original type — others evolving into bizarre perversions.

THE BIBLICAL HISTORY OF SACRIFICE

The account of animal sacrifice found in the Old Testament Book of Genesis occurred long before God gave the command to Moses to institute a system of worship which included animal sacrifices.

As noted above, the first innocent animal was sacrificed by God immediately after man and woman first sinned. From this God fashioned a skin covering for Adam and Eve's nakedness. They had attempted to cover themselves with leaves, but God rejected their feeble effort to hide their guilt from Him. In this, God established the principle that an innocent substitute must die to provide a temporary covering for man's sinfulness.

The skin coverings provided by God for them was the first picture of Christ clothing us with His righteousness. The sacrifice itself in both cases provides the clothing for our acceptance with God.

The sewing together of leaves to cover their sense of guilt was the first act of religion. Religion is always man's efforts to make himself acceptable to God by his own works.

Although this is not spelled out in detail by Moses in his writing of the Book of Genesis, it's obvious from succeeding records of animal sacrifice that God must have explained this substitutionary-death concept to Adam, and then Adam to his children.

Genesis records the fact that Abel, Noah, Abraham, Isaac, Job, and Jacob all offered sacrifices to God before the time of Moses and the institution of the tabernacle worship (Genesis 4:4; 8:20; 12:7; 26:25; 33:20; Exodus 12:3-11; Job 1:5; 42:7-9).

So the necessity of seeking God's forgiveness of sins through the sacrifice of an innocent substitute was a familiar practice from the very beginning of man's history on this earth. And it was a symbolism instituted by God Himself.

It's also thrilling to me to see how God developed the concept of the substitutionary death of *one lamb for one man* to the ultimate goal of *one lamb for the whole world.*

ONE LAMB FOR ONE MAN

God initially authorized the slaying of one animal to atone for the sins of one man. This is pictured for us in the story of Adam's son, Abel's sacrificial offering to God. His brother, Cain, brought an offering of fruit to God, but it was rejected. This was the second record of trying to be accepted by God through religion.

Obviously, God had previously given instructions through Adam that blood must be shed in order to provide a covering for sins. Abel brought the right sacrifice and was accepted. Cain's human efforts of religious works were rejected and it so angered him that he killed Abel. From Cain onward, religion has killed those who came by faith in God's way of salvation. The Inquisitions are just one example. (See also Genesis 3, 4; Hebrews 11:4.)

ONE LAMB FOR ONE FAMILY

In the story of the Passover experience of the Hebrews in Egypt we see that God ordained that one sacrificed lamb could atone for one family (Exodus 12:3-14).

The Passover referred to the night when God had Moses tell Pharaoh that if he didn't let the Hebrews go out of their slavery in Egypt, the first-born of all animals and families in the land (both Hebrew and Egyptian) would die as the death angel passed over Egypt.

In order to spare the Hebrews the death of their first-born, God made the provision that they could kill a lamb and sprinkle its blood over the door and on the two doorposts. Then when the death angel passed over the land of Egypt that night, wherever he saw the blood, he would *pass over* that house and those inside would be spared God's judgment.

God commanded that this Passover day be celebrated yearly as a reminder of God's provision for the salvation of those who sacrificed their lamb for their family.

ONE LAMB FOR A NATION

After the Jews left their servitude in Egypt and were on their way to the promised land, God met Moses on Mount Sinai and gave him the Ten Commandments and many other laws by which the people were to regulate their lives and their worship.

Principally, Moses was commanded to construct a portable building which was to be used in their worship and sacrificing to God. This was called the "Tabernacle."

It was made up of an outside court in which there was an altar for the animal sacrifices. There were two rooms on the inside. The first room was called the "Holy Place" and had several articles of furniture that were involved in the worship of God. The innermost room was the most important spot in the Tabernacle. It was called the "Holy of Holies," and it was where the Ark of the Covenant was kept and where the presence of God dwelt above the ark in a blaze of light called "Shekinah Glory."

It was in this Holy of Holies that God ordained that the blood of one sacrificial lamb could atone for the sins of the whole nation of Israel from year to year. It was the job of the high priest to select a perfect animal once a year and take the blood of it into the Holy of Holies and sprinkle it on the mercy seat. In so doing, it conciliated God's wrath against the nation for another year by atoning for the sins of the people. This day came to be called the "Day of Atonement" or Yom Kippor in Hebrew.

ONE LAMB FOR THE WORLD

Jesus' human cousin, John the Baptist, was the first person to call Jesus by the name "Lamb of God." When he saw Jesus coming toward him one day, he said, **"Behold, the Lamb of God who** *takes away* **the sin of the world"** (John 1:29).

Now, where do you suppose John got that mental picture of Jesus as a lamb, taking away the sins of the world?

No doubt in his knowledge of the Old Testament scriptures and his experience with animal sacrifice in the Temple in Jerusalem, he had come to realize that the continual shedding of the blood of substitutionary animals did not take away sins or the guilt they produced. He must have sensed that God had made some other provision for forgiveness and cleansing. I'm sure also that God must have supernaturally revealed to him that here was the One who would be that permanent provision for sin.

A few years after this incident with John and Jesus, the writer of the Book of Hebrews explained the whole reason why Jesus was called the "Lamb of God" who takes away the world's sins. I'm going to let him tell you in his own words, because he was obviously Jewish and had experienced some of the frustration of the empty religious treadmill of a sacrificial worship system that didn't really deal with the problem of sin.

You'll notice the number of times he contrasts the old way of doing things with a new one which Jesus instituted.

He makes very clear that the old system of approaching God through the blood of animals was never satisfactory to man or God. And then he convincingly sets forth the fact that Jesus was the permanent sacrifice that God had in mind all the time. This is all quoted from *The Living Bible*.

"The old system of Jewish laws gave only a dim foretaste of the good things The Messiah would do for us. The sacrifices under the old system were repeated again and again, year after year, but even so they could never save those who lived under their rules. If they could have, one offering would have been enough; the worshipers would have been cleansed once for all, and their feelings of guilt would be gone.

"But just the opposite happened: those yearly sacrifices reminded them of their disobedience and guilt instead of relieving their minds. For it is not possible for the blood of bulls and goats really to take away sins.

"That is why Christ said, as He came into the world, 'O, God, the blood of bulls and goats cannot satisfy you, so you have made ready this body of mine for me to lay as a sacrifice upon your altar. You were not satisfied with the animal sacrifices, slain and burnt before you as offerings for sin. Then I said, 'See, I have come to do your will, to lay down my life, just as the Scriptures said that I would.'

"After Christ said this, about not being satisfied with the various sacrifices and offerings required under the old system, he then added 'Here I am. I have come to give my life.'

"He cancels the first system in favor of a far better one. Under this new plan we have been forgiven and made clean by Christ's dying for us

once and for all. Under the old agreement the
priests stood before the altar day after day offering sacrifices that could never take away our sins.

"But Christ gave himself to God for our sins as
one sacrifice for all time, and then sat down in the
place of highest honor at God's right hand, waiting for his enemies to be laid under his feet. For
by that one offering he made forever perfect in the
sight of God all those whom he is making holy"
(Hebrews 10:1-14, TLB).

JESUS DIED TWICE

When Jesus was hanging on the cross as our substitute, the writer of Hebrews tells us, it was that **"He might
taste death for every one"** (Hebrews 2:9). Since man's
penalty for being a sinner is both spiritual and physical death,
Jesus had to taste both kinds of death.

When He shouted out, **"My God, My God, why
have You forsaken Me?"** at that moment, there on the cross,
He was actually made sin for us, and in His human nature He
died spiritually.

The Apostle Paul referred to this when he said, **"He
made Him** [Jesus] **who knew no sin *to be sin on our behalf,
that we might become the righteousness of God in Him"**
(2 Corinthians 5:21).

This doesn't mean Jesus was actually sinful in
Himself. It means He was treated by the Father as if He were
actually sinful. Since Jesus was bearing our sins, God had to
judge Him just as He would have had to judge us because of
our sins.

In dying spiritually and physically as our substitute,
God looked at Jesus' death and credited it to the account of

the fallen human race. His spiritual death means God can give spiritual life to all men who will receive it; and His physical death — and the defeat of His physical death by the resurrection — set God free to justly raise our physical bodies and give them immortality. (This is grace heaped upon grace.)

GOD'S ULTIMATE LAMB

There's little more that can be said to amplify this vivid picture of Jesus' substitutionary death on our behalf. The only thing to add is that in becoming a Lamb for the world's sins, Jesus *fulfilled the need* for one lamb for a man, one lamb for a family, and one lamb for a nation.

It was no mere coincidence that His crucifixion took place on the day of Passover. He was destined by God to be the world's Passover Lamb whose blood, when applied to the doorposts of our hearts, would cause God to "pass over" us in judgment. As Jesus assured, **"He who believes in Him is not judged..."** (John 3:18).

He was also the fulfillment of the lamb on the Day of Atonement upon whom the sins of the people were laid and who was slain in their behalf.

WHY?

The only question that might come to mind is, "Why did He do it?"

Jesus gave us the answer to that question when He told His disciples, **"Greater love has no one than this, that one lay down his life for his friends"** (John 15:13).

Jesus died for us because He loved us!

CHAPTER 12

RECONCILIATION

To me one of the happiest words in the English language is "reconciliation." I immediately picture two people being restored into a new relationship.

It's one of God's favorite words too, because it means He can now restore man into fellowship with Himself because of the sum total of the threefold work of Christ on the cross:

—*Propitiation* brings man out from under the wrath of God through satisfying His righteousness and justice.

—*Redemption* brings man out from slavery to sin and Satan through the payment of a ransom.

—*Substitutionary death* brings man out from under the penalty of death through the death of Christ in our place.

These three aspects of what Christ accomplished at the cross have torn down the barrier that man's sin built up against God. But even with the *barriers* removed, the *relationship* between God and man must be re-established. This is Christ's work of reconciliation.

It is important to remember that God never changed; He has always loved man and still does. The world has not changed either; it's still in rebellion against God. But what has changed is that judicially the barrier is now down, and when anyone sees this and *believes* Christ did it for him, he immediately becomes reconciled to God.

To put this great truth in the most simple way, RECONCILIATION means that God isn't angry with us anymore,

and He no longer holds our sins against us. The Lord Jesus
has borne all the anger God had against my sins and against
me, the sinner — He paid for them once and for all. So God
now deals with me in unmerited love or grace. God's wrath
will never be toward me again because it was all taken out on
Christ in my place. When I found that God wasn't angry at
me anymore, I stopped running from Him and turned to Him.
This is called reconciliation.

Reconciliation brings a man out from under his mental attitude of *alienation from God.* With the barrier taken out
of the way through the work of Christ on the cross, reconciliation means that, through Christ, man may now be brought
from alienation to fellowship with God. In fact, it's when man
really begins to see how Christ has so completely removed
the barrier so that He's no longer angry, that he begins to open
up toward God and want to be reconciled to Him.

THE GREEKS HAVE A WORD FOR IT!

You've heard the statement, "The Greeks have a
word for it." The Greek language has many words to every
one in the English. It was the most explicit language ever
devised in the history of the human race. I'm sure it's no mere
accident that this was the language God chose for the writing
of the New Testament.

There are three words in the Greek language express-
ing the idea of reconciliation, and all are translated by the one
English word "reconciliation."

WORD NO. 1

The word *daillassomai* (δαιλλασσομαι) means to
change two people to friendship who are both at odds with

each other. It's used that way in Matthew 5:24. **"...first be reconciled to your brother, and then come and present your offering."** These two people have turned their backs on each other; both are angry and need to be reconciled.

This word is *never* used with reference to God — we have turned our backs on God, not He on us!

WORD NO. 2

The second word for reconciliation is *apokatallasso* (αποκαταλλασσο). It's closely aligned with the main verb we want to consider. It means to change from enmity to fellowship permanently. This word also means that *only one person is alienated and needs to be reconciled.* The other person still loves the alienated one and needs no reconciliation. This is the word used with reference to man being reconciled to God forever. God never needed to be reconciled, **"For God so loved the world that He gave His only begotten Son, that whoever believes in Him should not perish, but have eternal life"** (John 3:16).

WORD NO. 3

This is the word I will spend the most time considering: *katallasso* (καταλλασσο). This word also means to change from enmity to fellowship. It is used several places in the New Testament. It's used throughout 2 Corinthians 5:17-21, the key passage on reconciliation.

Katallasso (reconciliation) views it this way: man is alienated with God; he's turned his back on God. God never had to be reconciled, He has always sought to bring man back. Man is running from God because of guilt, and this guilt has produced a state of alienation toward God. Man believes God hates him. *Katallasso* focuses on God removing man's alienation and bringing him into fellowship.

HOSEA AND THE HOOKER

The perfect example of the story of reconciliation is the Old Testament Book of Hosea, especially the first few chapters. I call this account the "Romance of Reconciliation." Here's why.

God told Hosea to marry a certain woman He had picked out for him. The woman God chose was a prostitute. Hosea married her and treated her with love and respect. She bore his children.

Then one day she ran off from him and returned to being a prostitute. God told Hosea to go and find her and bring her back.

He finally found his wife on the block at a slave auction. She stood there at the mercy of the bidders, stripped naked for all to view — the custom of the day for the auctioning of female slaves — waiting to be sold into slavery. Hosea bought back his own wife, clothed her, brought her back home, and kept right on loving her with no recrimination.

What a picture! Hosea learned experientially just how God felt about Israel, how Israel's love affairs with pagan gods hurt Him, and how He would stop at nothing to bring these people back.

But this is also a picture of what all of us have done to God and of what God has done to bring us back. It's a picture of God's kind of love. You see, Hosea never stopped loving his wife; it was she who turned from him. And the idea is given that Hosea's great love absolutely overwhelmed his wife. She couldn't get over the fact that he still loved her.

As a picture of reconciliation, the Book of Hosea is a Rembrandt!

God never had to be reconciled! He's like Hosea. But it's man who has to be brought back and reconciled, and this is what the word *katallasso* means.

Like Hosea, God knew we would never be brought back to Him unless (a) God took the initiative and (b) God took us "just as we are" in our condition of sin. Hosea didn't try to clean up his wife before he brought her home, nor did she try to clean herself up. She came just as she was and the clean-up took place later. She never would have wanted to come home if she thought that Hosea was going to hold what she had done against her.

I'm sure Gomer, Hosea's wife, must have been filled with guilt and shame when she heard Hosea bidding for her at the slave auction. After he got her home, her sense of unworthiness and guilt probably produced an attitude of suspicion and alienation toward Hosea, wondering when he was going to get even with her.

But as the days went by and all that Gomer got from Hosea was love and acceptance, her hostility turned to love and gratitude and she became his loveslave. The reconciler's love is what melts away the alienation of the sinner.

RECONCILIATION NEUTRALIZES HOSTILITY

True reconciliation always does away with hostility. That's what the Apostle Paul was speaking of when he said, **"And although you were *formerly* alienated and hostile in mind, engaged in evil deeds, yet He has now reconciled you in His fleshly body through death..."** (Colossians 1:21,22).

If we think someone is holding something against us, then we'll feel alienated and hostile toward them, simply out of self-defense. It's even more true when it comes to God. If we feel our sins are still an issue between us and God, then we won't feel like coming to Him because we know how He feels about sin.

But listen to this terrific good news from the pen of the Apostle Paul: **"God was in Christ reconciling the world to Himself,** *not counting their trespasses against them,* **and He has committed to us the word of reconciliation"** (2 Corinthians 5:19).

Did you get it? God isn't holding our sins against us anymore. The reconciliation He made available to us through the cross has neutralized His just anger at our sins.

That's why the "cross" must always be the central message of the Gospel, because it's what Christ did there that makes reconciliation with God possible. And without reconciliation there's no way to remove the alienation and hostility that we have in our minds toward God.

When we find out how totally God has done away with the barrier that separated us from Him, and that He isn't mad at us, then we're going to want to "come home" like Hosea's wife did. And when we "come home," we're so grateful for the lack of recrimination and the complete acceptance, that all we want to do is serve our Master.

THE WAYWARD SON COMES HOME

Another beautiful illustration of reconciliation is the parable that Jesus told about the prodigal son (Luke 15).

It's important to get the setting of this incident or a great deal of its meaning is lost. Jesus was teaching, and the biggest part of His audience were tax-gatherers and self-admitted sinners. Interspersed among them were some of the pious super-religious Pharisees and scribes, and they began to make snide remarks about Jesus' friendship with sinners.

Jesus tells three parables to this group. His purpose was to teach God's attitude toward those who recognize they are sinners. You see, the Pharisees were sinners, but they didn't think they were. So Jesus was trying to show them that it's better to admit you're a sinner and place yourself under God's grace, than to bravely defend your self-righteousness and miss out on God's grace.

In this particular parable of the prodigal or wayward son, there was a father with two sons. The younger one decided he wanted his inheritance so he could leave home and live it up (he represents the publicans and sinners). The older son (representing the self-righteous Pharisees) stayed at home and continued to work for his father (who represents God in this story).

The younger son went into a far-off country and squandered all his inheritance with wild living. A severe famine came in that land, and he found himself in real need. So he hired out to a certain citizen and found himself out in the fields feeding pigs (this citizen was Satan).

Finally the boy said to himself, "This is ridiculous! I'm here starving while my father's slaves have better food than this. I will go to my father and tell him, 'Father, I know I've sinned against heaven and you by the stupid way I've blown my inheritance, and I'm not even worthy to be a son of yours. But if you'll let me come home, I'll be glad just to be one of your servants.'"

You can tell by what he said that he expected his father to have nothing to do with him after the way he'd disappointed him. But he was in for a big surprise!

While he was still a long way from his father's house, his dad caught sight of him. It's obvious the father must have been hopefully keeping an eye out for him ever since he left. And when he saw him, he ran to the son and threw his arms around him and kissed him.

Then the boy began the speech he'd planned about not being worthy, and being willing to come home as a hired man.

But the father never heard a word he said, for he was already giving instructions to the servants to get a big wel-come-home party ready. There was no resentment or wrath in the father toward that boy, even though there was plenty of reason for him to be upset.

The father's attitude was expressed in his statement to everyone, **"This son of mine was dead and has come to life again; he was lost, and has been found"** (Luke 15:24).

RECONCILIATION ISN'T "REASONABLE"

This parable is such a terrific illustration of reconcili-ation. Obviously this father dearly loved this boy all his life or he never would have given him his inheritance before it was due, as he had asked. During all those long months and possibly years, the father kept on loving the boy and yearning for him to come home and be reconciled to him.

When the boy recognized how foolish he'd been, he expected there to be stern barriers between him and his father if he wanted to come home. But when he got to the place of willingness to come back to his dad, he found that instead of being barriers, there was nothing but love and complete acceptance.

DON'T MISS THE POINT

There are certain very important truths which this parable teaches, but there are also some very strong things it *doesn't* teach.

First, keep in mind that it is a parable. This was one of Jesus' favorite teaching devices. A parable has one basic point. By contrast, each part of an allegory can be applied to real life. Not so with a parable. An example of an allegory is the Vine and the Branches of John chapter 15.

In this parable of the prodigal son, the most important thing it *doesn't* teach is that we're all sons of God, some of whom have simply gone astray. The persons represented by the wayward son were the self-admitted sinners, and these were people who still needed to get right with God.

All men are *creatures* of God and, as such, the objects of His love. Man was once in a relationship of intimacy with God, but has been in a position of straying and rebellion since Adam's fall. And the fact that the father says of his son that he was "dead and is now alive, was lost and is now found" shows that a very radical change had taken place in the relationship of these two.

The change that had taken place is called "reconciliation."

BE YE RECONCILED! ! !

But reconciliation is worth nothing unless the barriers that caused it in the first place are torn down, and then the one who is alienated decides to become reconciled. The prodigal son had to decide to renounce the rebellious life he'd chosen and to go home. That's simply called "repenting," which means to "change your mind and your direction."

Hosea's wife had run from him, but when he came to get her, she had to be willing to go back home with him.

By these four mighty works of Christ on the cross...

propitiation (1 John 2:2),

redemption (1 Timothy 2:5,6),

substitutionary death (Hebrews 2:9),

reconciliation (2 Corinthians 5:19)...

...God has made all men "reconcilable," but the effect of these truths becomes a reality only when a person believes them. 1 Timothy 4:10 says, **"We have fixed our hope on the living God, who is the Savior of all men,** *especially of* *believers.***"**

Just how a person becomes personally reconciled to God is a matter of the greatest importance. Our whole eternal destiny depends upon the right decision in this matter. The next chapter will carefully discuss this most important question we must answer: "Have I personally been reconciled to God?"

CHAPTER 13

THE DECISION
OF DESTINY

In the last four chapters we saw the wonders of God's grace that removed all the barriers between Himself and man.

But the really incredible thing is that God has purchased a total pardon for even those human beings whom He knew would reject it.

God so loved the "world" that He gave His Son (John 3:16). Christ didn't die for just part of the world, but for the whole world. It was for all of those who would ridicule His name, ignore His salvation, despise His Word, and reject His authority.

Whether they want to be or not, the whole world has been made "savable" because of the death of Christ on the cross.

But being "savable" and being "saved" are two different things.

If someone has put $1,000,000 in a bank account for you, it won't do you any good unless, first of all, you know about it; and, second, you draw upon it.

The four great doctrines of Christ's death in man's behalf are for the whole world, but applicable only to those who draw upon it personally.

—Propitiation: "He Himself [Jesus] is the propitiation for our sins; and not for ours only, *but also for those of the whole world*" (1 John 2:2).

—**Redemption:** "**For there is one God, and one mediator also between God and men, the man Christ Jesus, who gave Himself as** *a ransom for all*" (1 Timothy 2:5,6).

—**Substitutionary Death:** "**But we do see Him who has been made for a little while lower than the angels, namely, Jesus, because of the suffering of death crowned with glory and honor, that by the grace of God, He might** *taste death for every one*" (Hebrews 2:9).

—**Reconciliation:** "**God was in Christ** *reconciling the world to Himself*, **not counting their trespasses against them...**" (2 Corinthians 5:19).

I once heard a speaker liken God's worldwide offer of salvation to a petstore owner who puts a free kitten in the window of his shop. It's *available* to everyone, but it only becomes the possession of the one who goes in and claims it.

God has put His offer of "free forgiveness" in His window and it's available to everyone, but only the possession of those who come in and take it.

DON'T GET THE CART BEFORE THE HORSE!

Now in light of the fact the barriers have been removed from between God and man, and God freely offers man a new relationship, what must a person do to receive the results of this and have it become a reality?

At no other point is it more important to distinguish between the *means* of coming into God's salvation and the *results* of salvation. It's of utmost importance that we don't get the cart before the horse in the matter of *how* to appropriate all that Christ accomplished for us on the cross.

If we make something which the Bible calls a *result* of salvation part of the *means* by which it's obtained, then we insert human merit into God's redemptive plan. And human merit *nullifies* the whole concept of a *free* salvation. As Paul warned, **"For if those who are of the Law are heirs, *faith* is made void and the promise is nullified; for the Law brings about wrath, but where there is no law, neither is there violation. For this reason it is by *faith*, that it might be in accordance with *grace...*"** (Romans 4:14-16). The Law is a system that depends on human merit.

Now let's take a look at some of the things that men have tried to add to "faith" as an additional means of salvation.

FAITH, PLUS WORKS?

The Apostle Paul, knowing that all men have an insatiable self-centeredness that makes them want to boast of their spiritual or moral prowess, wrote to the believers in Ephesus, **"For by *grace* you have been saved through faith; and *that not of yourselves,* it is the gift of God; *not as a result of works,* that no one should boast"** (Ephesians 2:8,9).

It's a real commentary on the nature of the human heart that at the very outset of Christianity, Paul had to admonish people that salvation is a free gift from God and there's no possible way to do anything to merit it, or else human pride and boasting would come in. There will be all kinds of sinners in heaven, but there will be no boasters.

You see, if God required anything of man in the way of good deeds or human effort in order to receive God's salvation, then there would be good reason for some people to boast about how they helped God save them. But this is the real issue — the moment human merit is introduced into the equation, the standard for salvation becomes, **"Therefore you shall be perfect, just as your Father in heaven is perfect"** (Matthew 5:48 NKJV).   Breathes there a person so arrogant as to really think he can be as perfect as God? I have run into a surprising number who think they can be. They haven't graduated from God's Law School yet.

G.R.A.C.E.: GOD'S RICHES AT CHRIST'S EXPENSE

But over and over we keep running into a word in the New Testament that tells us the true basis on which God accepts us. That word is GRACE.

If we could have only a half-dozen words in our human vocabulary, that word should be one of them. It's one of those words that's so loaded with meaning, I feel as if I need a book just to begin to explain it. (Well, I hope this book helps.)

But simply put, it means to *freely give something to someone which he can in no possible way deserve, merit or earn.*

The instant there's even a hint of someone trying to merit or earn the thing being given, then it no longer can be given by grace. The Holy Spirit brought out the mutual exclusiveness of grace and works or human merit, **"And if by grace, then it is no longer by works; if it were, grace would no longer be grace"** (Romans 11:6 NIV).

Now, what is it that God has given to us that we can't in any way merit?

His righteousness, love, forgiveness, acceptance, mercy, redemption, inheritance and etrnal life — all of which are wrapped up in one package called "salvation." This is what He's given to us, if we'll take it, and it's given completely on the basis of "grace."

My first brush, on the human level, with the concept of grace was when I got my first health insurance policy. After paying ten hard-earned bucks a month for a couple of years on this policy, I came to a place where I just couldn't scrape together ten dollars one month. I hated to let the policy lapse, because I'd paid so much on it already and I'd never used it once.

But when the payment date arrived, I just didn't send them anything and I sadly figured that would be the last I'd hear of them. Yet, after a couple of weeks I got a letter from them telling me that my policy hadn't been canceled and I was in a thirty-day "grace" period.

I didn't deserve that thirty extra days of coverage, and I hadn't paid for it, but I found out that I was fully covered anyway in case any sickness or accident had happened to me.

That was only human grace, so you can imagine what divine grace must be like.

GRACE IS GOD'S PART: FAITH IS MAN'S!

If you had a present for someone you loved and he kept trying to do something to earn it, you'd feel rebuffed in your effort to show your unreserved affection. If you wanted him to work for the present, then it wouldn't really be a gift—it would be a wage.

That's what Paul says about man's efforts to work for God's favor: **"Now when a man works, his wages are not credited to him as a gift, but as an obligation. However, to the man who does not work but trusts God who justifies the wicked, his faith is credited as righteousness"** (Romans 4:4,5 NIV).

Nothing could be more clear.

A man's *faith* in what Jesus freely made available to him at the cross by *grace* is what God credits to his account as righteousness.   He exchanges my faith for His righteousness.

YEAH, BUT...!

The "cart-before-the-horse-crowd" is probably bursting right now with all kinds of "Yes, buts...! And what about the Book of James that says that "faith without works is dead"?

There's one thing for sure: if James meant that faith and works *together* constitute salvation (as some believe he means), then his teaching is in diametric opposition to everything God taught through Paul. Now, since I don't believe the Bible can contradict itself, let's take a good look at what James was really teaching.

THE MAN FROM MISSOURI

In chapter two, James is addressing a group of people who claim to be true believers in Jesus but don't manifest any evidence of this fact in their lives. So James takes the position that faith can only be seen *by men* through what it produces in a life. He gives two completely different biblical case histories to prove this point and to show that true faith always produces evidence of its genuineness.

CASE NO. 1: ABRAHAM

The first case James mentions is that of Abraham when God called upon him to be willing to offer up his dearly loved and only son, Isaac, as a burnt sacrifice. In complete obedience and trust that God knew what He was doing,

Abraham actually went so far as to place Isaac onto an altar and raise a knife to cut his throat. But God stopped Abraham at the last moment. God saw what He wanted to see. Abraham loved God even more than the son God had given him. This demonstration of faith proved that he was the man God could use to be the father of a race of people called the "Hebrews."

But it is very important to note that this testing in Abraham's life, recorded in Genesis 22, happened forty years *after* God had already declared Abraham righteous on the basis of his faith alone. Genesis 15:6 records the conversation that God initially had with Abraham when He told him that he would have many descendants. Abraham was about seventy-five years old then, and he was childless. Abraham couldn't figure out how he could be the father of so many nations, when he remained childless for twenty-five more years after the promise.

It was this simple faith in God's promise that caused God to count Abraham as righteous. From that day until the time he actually took his son to Mount Moriah to offer him as a sacrifice, nearly forty years transpired. Many times during that period Abraham failed God. But one thing stood sure in all those years — he was still considered righteous before God on the basis of his act of faith recorded in Genesis 15:6.

The main point is it took God forty years to mature Abraham's faith to the level we see in Genesis chapter 22.

After giving this illustration of Abraham's faith in offering up Isaac, James says about this, **"*You see* that a man is justified by works, and not by faith alone"** (James 2:24).

It's true that *man* sees the works. But it's also true that God *saw* Abraham's faith forty years before and on that basis pronounced him unconditionally righteous (Genesis 15; Romans 4:1-5).

The point is that after forty years of being declared as

righteous as God, Abraham was taught by God how to believe in the impossible. But faith was the *means* of his salvation, and works were the *results* of God's work in him.

True faith will always produce works. But works will never produce true faith. Get the point? God gives us a new nature that always wants to follow Him. Then He empowers us as we learn to believe Him moment by moment. Then man can see the results.

CASE NO. 2: RAHAB THE HARLOT

Lest we get the idea that in order to be declared righteous by God we must have some enormous demonstration of faith as Abraham did, James gives another case history to show how little a thing is evidence enough to show true faith.

At a time in Israel's history when she was seeking to enter the Promised Land, spies were sent from the wandering nation of Israel into Jericho to see what kind of opposition they would encounter if they tried to enter. Two Hebrew spies entered the home of a harlot named Rahab, and although she was a Gentile and didn't know these two men, she hid them from her fellow countrymen when they came looking for the spies (Joshua 2:1-7).

After their pursuers were gone, Rahab told the Hebrew spies that her whole nation had heard about the Red Sea opening up for them forty years earlier. And how all the people of Jericho had lived in fear of the nation of Israel because of the great things their God had done for them in bringing them out of captivity in Egypt.

Then this Gentile prostitute said, "**...for the Lord your God, He is God in heaven above and on earth beneath. Now therefore, please swear to me by the Lord,**

since I have dealt kindly with you, that you also will deal kindly with my father's household [when you come in to conquer the land]" (Joshua 2:11,12).

Now, this doesn't seem like much of a work, but it was enough to show that she had come to believe in the God of Israel and that *faith* prompted her to hide Israel's spies from her countrymen.

From both these illustrations of James it can be seen that faith is only as good as its object, and the object must be God and confidence in His power and His word. When whatever faith we have, whether it be great like Abraham's or small like Rahab's, is placed in God, then there will be the resulting evidence in our lives, because His Spirit will work through us.

If there are never any righteous works in a person's life, then it well may be that there is no true faith. But if there is true faith, I guarantee you there will be good deeds eventually. The new nature plus the indwelling Holy Spirit will produce evidence of life.

FAITH, PLUS REPENTANCE?

Whenever we add anything to the one necessary ingredient of "faith" in order to receive God's salvation and sanctification, then we're in danger of getting that cart in front of the horse again. Some people put a big stress on repentance as a necessary condition for receiving reconciliation. To be sure, repentance is definitely involved in becoming a child of God, but it must be carefully defined.

There are those who, in their zeal to get people to turn from their sinful ways and receive the Lord, almost put repentance on a par with believing. Repentance is defined by them as a deep sorrow over sin, usually evidenced by weeping and/or much emotion.

This is a faulty understanding of the word "repentance." It's certainly all right to have a deep emotional sorrow about having spent a life rejecting Christ, but that's not all that's involved in repentance.

Judas Iscariot felt such sorrow about betraying Jesus that he wept uncontrollably and even returned the money he had received for betraying Him to His enemies. But he never repented or believed. Instead, he hung himself as a result of utter despair from guilt (see Matthew 27:3-5).

When we're talking with someone about his need for Christ, we need to find out where his head is about the matter of sin. If he doesn't realize that he's a sinner, then he will not know that he needs a Savior. In a case like that it is necessary to emphasize God's view of sin and seek to show the person that according to the Bible's definition, he qualifies as a sinner.

But the emphasis should *not* be upon the man's personal sins—such as lying, cheating, adultery, dope, or what have you—with an effort to try to get him to feel bad for doing those things. The emphasis should be upon what God has done to remove all the barriers that separate God and man, including the barrier of sin. What Jesus did for him should be the focus.

TO CHANGE, OR NOT TO CHANGE!
THAT'S THE QUESTION!

The word repentance, *metanoeo* (μετανοεω) in the Greek, means to have a *change of mind* toward something or someone. It means a turning around from one attitude to another which produces a change in direction. It's a word related to our reason, rather than to our emotions, although whatever deeply affects our reason will also touch our emotions. But the driving force of true repentance is reason and will, not emotion.

Repentance, as it relates to Christ, means to change our minds about Him, who He is and what He has done to provide forgiveness and deliverance from our sins. When we place faith in Jesus as having taken our place personally on the cross and borne the penalty due our sins, then we automatically repent, because we couldn't accept Him in this way without changing our minds concerning Him.

The essence of the issue is this: *you can repent and not believe; but you can't believe and not repent.* This is why in the Gospel of John, which was expressly written to bring people to new life in Christ, the condition "believe in Christ" is stated ninety-nine times. But the word "repent" isn't used at all in the book.

You may wonder why I've made an issue of this. I am an evangelist. I have seen all kinds of people believe in Jesus as Savior and go on to be productive Christians. But I've also seen people make a decision and receive Christ as Savior. Then later, because they didn't have some deep emotional experience of regret over their sins, then doubt whether their belief was sincere enough to save them.

Let me tell you right now, if while you've been reading this book, you've said to yourself, "This is true and I believe it. I don't understand it all, but I believe what I do understand," then I guarantee you that you've become a child of God. Whether your faith is strong like Abraham's or weak like Rahab's, it makes no difference. You've placed it in the right object by putting it in Christ. It is not the power of your faith, but the power of the One in Whom you placed your faith that saves you.

FAITH, PLUS THE LORDSHIP OF CHRIST?

This is a very subtle form of human merit which some add to "faith" as a condition of salvation. It's another "cart before the horse," and this one presents a tremendous problem, because it's an open-ended, indefinable condition.

For instance, who can say at this moment, no matter how long he's been a believer, that he has *everything* in his life under the lordship of Jesus? Most believers would like to have that be true. But as long as we still have our unreformable sin natures, the world system and the Devil all working against us, we are not likely to reach total perfection.

If even mature believers are conscious of areas of their lives that aren't always in submission to Christ, how can we make an unbeliever responsible to do something as a condition of salvation that mature Christians are still not able to do?

Those who say, "If Christ is not Lord of all, He's not Lord at all" have a good sounding slogan, but they're laying a burden on the potential believer that is impossible to bear. But worse than that, they're subtly adding "works" to faith which nullifies grace and makes salvation impossible.

It is a very serious matter to make expensive that which cost God the death of His beloved Son to make free.

The scriptural teaching on this issue is that we must recognize Jesus as Lord in the sense He is not just a man, but the Lord from heaven who became a man to die for our sins. Yet even this understanding doesn't fully come until we have believed in Him as Savior and received new spiritual life so that we have the facility for understanding spiritual truth.

There's nothing wrong with telling an interested seeker that Christ wants to be his Lord once He comes to live within him, but unless that information is coupled with the

teaching regarding the Holy Spirit's indwelling power to progressively make Jesus Lord of his life, it's better not to bring
it up. Once the person is saved, the Holy Spirit Himself will
bring up the issue of Christ's Lordship.

The Apostle Paul taught what is necessary to be
saved, **"If you confess with your mouth Jesus as Lord, and
believe in your heart that God raised Him from the dead,
you shall be saved; for with the heart man believes, resulting in righteousness, and with the mouth he confesses,
resulting in salvation"** (Romans 10:9-10).

Two ingredients of salvation are mentioned in these
verses. One is a *cause* and the other is an *effect*. One has to
do with the heart or mind, and the other has to do with the
mouth.

Look at the verses carefully. Paul says that what a
man believes with his heart about Christ's resurrection will
result in God giving him Christ's righteousness. That's another way of saying that the man has just become a child of God.

Then it teaches that with the mouth he is to confess
Jesus Christ is the Lord and his own personal Savior.

The believing is the *cause* of salvation, and the *effect*
is the confession of Jesus as the Lord. It's our faith in His
saving work, not His supremacy, that saves us.

FAITH, PLUS BAPTISM?

The adding of a God-ordained ritual to faith as a condition of salvation down through the dark history of God's
dealing with man has been one of the most subtle errors. The
issue of water baptism has been the most confusing, since
Jesus himself commanded this ritual (Matthew 28:19,20) and
the Book of Acts shows that this was the common practice of
believers.

There's no question that a believer who's had the real meaning of water baptism explained to him will want to be baptized after receiving Christ as Savior. The rite of baptism is the believer's testimony to God and the world that he believes he's been totally identified with Christ in His death, burial, and resurrection. In baptism we express our faith that we are now raised with Jesus into a new life where sin has no right to rule over him.

It's been particularly thrilling to me to see the way thousands of people today have desired to express in this dramatic, tangible way the fact that they have come to believe in Christ as their Savior. No one has laid any big trip on these people about the necessity of being baptized. But strangely enough, once they understand that they have been joined to Christ, they want to jump into the nearest ocean, lake, or swimming pool and publicly announce that they belong to Christ.

But as beautiful and as meaningful as this necessary symbol is, it still must be seen as a *result* of salvation, not a *cause* of it, or even a partial cause of it. If we add baptism as a condition of being saved, then it becomes a work and an act of human merit which nullifies grace.

AN OLD ERROR, REVIVED

Most of the Jews in Jesus' time made the same error as some believers do today. The ritual of circumcision given to them through Abraham corresponded to the ritual of water baptism today.

This teaching of the necessity of adding circumcision to faith was the source of a great controversy in the early church (Acts 15:1-11). The Apostle Paul, in demonstrating that salvation has always been by faith alone, selected two of the greatest men in the Old Testament as an illustration of that fact: Abraham and David.

Read carefully what Paul says of Abraham: **"If Abraham was justified by works, he has something to boast about; but not before God. For what does the Scripture say? 'Abraham *believed* God, and it was reckoned to him as righteousness'"** (Romans 4:2,3).

Then Paul shows that Abraham's justification before God on the basis of faith was apart from any ritual: **"Is this blessing then upon the circumcised, or upon the uncircumcised also? For we say, 'Faith was reckoned to Abraham as righteousness.' How then was it reckoned? While he was circumcised, or uncircumcised?"** And then Paul answers his own question, **_"Not while circumcised, but while uncircumcised;_ and he received the sign of circumcision, a seal of the righteousness of the faith which he had while uncircumcised"** (Romans 4:9-11).

Paul argues relentlessly on this point, because any ritual, be it circumcision, communion, or baptism, when it is added to faith as a condition of salvation, it becomes a work of human merit. And that is totally incompatible with grace.

PAUL WASN'T SENT TO BAPTIZE

Paul shows that baptism clearly isn't a condition of salvation when he says, **"I thank God that I baptized none of you, except Crispus and Gaius, that no man should say you were baptized in my name."**

And then he suddenly remembers some others he'd baptized and so he adds, **"Now I did baptize also the household of Stephanas; beyond that, I do not know whether I**

baptized any other. For Christ did not send me to baptize, but to preach the gospel, not in cleverness of speech, that the cross of Christ should not be made void" (1 Corinthians 1:14-17).

Though Paul had led most of the Corinthian church to Christ, he couldn't remember too well whom he had baptized. Then he makes a colossal statement, **"Christ did not send me to baptize, but to preach the gospel."** Paul's mission in life was to bring people into the salvation of Jesus Christ. If baptism were an integral part of salvation, then he could never have made the above statement. Paul would have practically pulled a portable baptistry around behind him if baptism was a condition of the Gospel of salvation.

Instead, Paul concentrated on the one thing: preaching the gospel. Because when men believe it, it is the power of God that brings salvation (Romans 1:16,17).

THE REAL ISSUE IS FAITH, PLUS NOTHING!

God has always had only one way of saving men, and that's been on the basis of **"grace…through faith…not as a result of works, that no one should boast"** about how he helped God save him (Ephesians 2:8,9).

Even in the Old Testament, salvation was by "grace, through faith." There was no man who could say he deserved God's forgiveness. All men deserved His condemnation, but before Christ came, God graciously provided the animal sacrifices to picture the coming Lamb of God who would take away the world's sins.

However, simply offering sacrifices didn't save a man. He had to come in faith, believing that this was God's provision at that time to atone for his sins, and he had to trust in God to graciously withhold his judgment from him as long as he brought his offerings in faith.

The New Testament also clearly teaches that faith is the *means* of salvation. There are many *results*. Among them will be good deeds, repentance, Christ progressively becoming the Lord of your life, baptism, obedience, service, the fruits of the Spirit, spiritual gifts, and on and on.

But the issue that must remain central is that faith alone is all that's necessary for salvation. Remember the thief on the cross beside Jesus. He believed in Christ while nailed to a cross in the process of dying. He couldn't come down from the cross and do any good deeds, he couldn't be baptized, and he couldn't go out and manifest the Christian life to the world by holy living.

Nevertheless, Jesus told him that before the day ended he would be in paradise with him because he had believed on Jesus.

I'm aware of the fact that some teach that God has had different ways of saving man at different times in human history. But if God ever compromised and made an exceptional case out of even one man's salvation, He would be honor-bound by His own character to do it for all.

God's attribute of justice demands that He be equitable and fair with everyone, for as Paul points out in Romans 2:11, **"there is no partiality with God."** If God could save a thief by faith alone—and He did—then He must do it the same way for everyone.

Besides all this, if there had been some other way for man to be reconciled to God without God putting to death His own dear Son, don't you think God would have found it? But that death was necessary to remove every barrier that stood between God and man, so that God could deal with us in

grace. Having done all this, God is not going to impose conditions on us for salvation which involve human merit, thus
nullifying what cost Him an infinite price to make a free gift
to us.

MAKING OUR "WITHDRAWAL"

I said at the beginning of this chapter that if someone
deposited $1,000,000 in a bank account for you, it would be
of no benefit to you unless you knew about it and then withdrew it from the bank.

Now you know what it is that God has done for you
on the cross and how to draw upon it by faith alone.

The next move is up to you!

CHAPTER 14

JUSTIFICATION

T here is a story in the New Testament which so beautifully illustrates justification that I'm going to begin with it and wait a few pages to define the word. By the time you've digested this "Saga of Justification," little definition should be necessary.

A CLERGYMAN AND A TAX COLLECTOR (LUKE 18:9-14)

Two men went over to the Temple to pray. One was a super-religious do-gooder called a Pharisee. The other was a tax collector, called a Publican.

A tax man in those days was considered by the Pharisees, the religious crowd, to be the most wicked sinner in the world. He was a man who betrayed his own countrymen by collecting more taxes than were assigned by the government. This dishonest profit was the only payment for services he received; he didn't get a salary. He was told to keep everything "over and above." A Publican, then, made his money by extortion from his fellow citizens.

A Pharisee was a member of a Jewish religious order that went to the Temple three times a day and prayed on his own seven times daily. Talk about trying to pile up Brownie points with God! Then it says, **"The Pharisee stood and was praying thus to himself, 'God, I thank Thee that I am not like other people, swindlers, unjust, adulterers, or even like this** [ugh!] **tax-gatherer'"** (Luke 18:11). Then you

can just hear him ticking off all his good deeds to the Lord—
fasting, tithing, praying, sacrificing.

Do you think this guy was kidding?

No! He did all these things. Why, in the average
church today he'd be considered a real pillar, wouldn't he?
People would applaud him: "Look at this great saint of God."
Everything he did in the public eye was beyond reproach.

Then in verse 13, the other man prayed, **"God, be
merciful to me, the sinner."** It says he was unwilling even to
lift his eyes to heaven, but instead was beating his breast. This
"beating of the breast" was a sign of sorrow and unworthiness. He counted himself unworthy to come to God. His
prayer reflected that.

Let's look more carefully at this prayer for mercy.

The Greek word *hilastheti* (ἱλασθετι) used here
should never have been translated into the English word
"merciful" because it actually means "to be propitious." I'm
sure that the translators felt the word "merciful" was a more
familiar word to the English reader than the word "propitious," but theologically it does not connote the true meaning
of the word or the passage.

You see, God has never had to be persuaded to be
merciful. It was His mercy that caused Him to find a way to
satisfy His outraged holiness so that He could act toward us in
grace. When the tax-collector prayed to God and asked Him
to be "propitious" toward him, he was actually saying, "I
know you're not satisfied with *me*. I'm nothing but a no-
good sinner who only deserves Your just wrath. But please
receive me in the light of the atoning blood of sacrifice on the
mercy seat which has satisfied your judgment against me."

He may not have used those words, but when he
asked God to be propitious toward him, that's exactly what he
meant.

JESUS LOOKS AT THE HEART

What did Jesus say about this tax-collecting sinner? **"I tell you, this man went down to his house *justified* rather than the other; for everyone who exalts himself shall be humbled, but he who humbles himself shall be exalted."** (Luke 18:14).

To be humble means to have a true estimation of yourself and where you stand with God. To recognize there's nothing you can do to make yourself good enough for God's acceptance — that all you can do is throw yourself upon His grace.

By contrast, look at how the Pharisee approached God. He was full of pride about all the things he was *doing* to gain God's approbation. His deeds in themselves were not wrong, but his motive and method were. His pride gave away the fact that he didn't understand the real meaning of God's absolute righteousness nor His provision of a propitiation through sacrifice for his falling short of it.

JUSTIFICATION DEFINED

A simple definition which I've often heard for "justification" is *"just-as-if-I'd-never-sinned."* It makes a clever-sounding phrase, but unfortunately it only explains the negative half of justification.

Even though Christ has taken all my sins away, that only leaves me in a *neutral* status with God. Just having no sin will never make me acceptable in God's sight.

In order to be acceptable to God, I need more than just the *subtraction* of my sins. I need the *addition* of Christ's righteousness.

The Apostle Paul tells us how God arranged for this exchange. God made Christ **"...who knew no sin to be sin**

on our behalf, that we might become the righteousness of
God in Him" (2 Corinthians 5:21). In other words, God took
our sins and put them on Christ and then took Christ's righteousness and gave it to us in exchange.

That's what it means to be justified.

Because of the propitiation accomplished by Christ,
God is now free to instantly and irrevocably "declare righteous" any man, woman, or child who places faith in Christ as
Savior. God declares that person to be just as righteous in *His*
sight as His Son, Jesus Christ. This is our new "standing"
with God.

THE "MISINTERPRETATION" THAT SPLIT THE CHURCH

It's very important however, that the meaning of the
word "justify" as used in the New Testament be precisely
understood. There's a vast difference between being
"declared" righteous by God and actually "becoming" righteous in my daily behavior. The justification happens instantly
and totally the moment I believe in Christ. It forever settles
my acceptance and standing in eternity with God. He can
never again see me in any way except as having the righteousness of His Son.

However, my "becoming" righteous in my daily
behavior is a life-long process which begins at spiritual birth.
This process is called *progressive sanctification*. This continues as long as we are in this life on earth. But, whether I'm
making good progress in my daily sanctification or not, does
not alter my justification. God continues to see me as
absolutely righteous because He declared me so.

The biggest rift that ever developed in Christianity

grew out of a confusion of this very issue of the difference between being "declared" righteous and and "being made" righteous in behavior. This rift became known as *The Reformation.* It forced a re-focus on two greatly abused truths: *first,* that justification is exclusively an act of God based on the finished work of Christ's propitiatory sacrifice; and *second,* Christ's righteousness is received totally and irrevocably at the *moment* of salvation on the basis of FAITH ALONE.

LUTHER AND THE REFORMATION OF THE CHURCH

Salvation on the Installment Plan A German Augustinian monk of the Catholic Church, Martin Luther, was the catalyst that brought about the Reformation. The theology of his day taught that justification meant that when one professed belief in Christ, God declared all his *past* sins forgiven. But he must then enter into a life-long process of obtaining continued forgiveness and righteousness by his own religious performance. This included the necessity of such things as the attendance of Mass at church, good works, self denial, penance in the form of self-inflicted punishment and pain, prayers, confession, giving of money, and so forth.

In spite of careful performance of all these things, Luther wrestled continually with a sense of guilt and spiritual inadequacy. His superiors thought that he would perhaps be better as a teacher in the seminary than doing pastoral work. After all, with his constant severe guilt problem, he couldn't help the people very much.

As the providence of God would have it, Luther was assigned to teach the Greek New Testament. As he studied

and taught the Books of Romans and Galatians, he encountered an even more disturbing problem. He found it impossible to reconcile the clear teaching of the original Greek versions of Romans and Galatians with Church tradition.

Finally, in desperation, his superiors thought a pil-
grimage to the mother Church in Rome would convince this
troubled monk that the Church was right in its traditional doctrine. Luther performed an act of penance and pain (called a
Novena) which he thought might ease his troubled mind.
While crawling on his knees up the steps of the Church in
Rome, the strangest thing happenned. As if it were written
across the sky in fire, he saw this verse from the Epistle to the
Romans, **"The *just* shall live by *faith*"** (Romans 1:17 KJV).

There was no way Luther could equate what he was
doing at that moment with living by faith. He was living by
works and seeking to improve his righteousness in God's eyes
by his own human merits.

In that instant the Reformation was born. Luther got
up from his knees and with pen and preaching began to liberate hundreds of thousands of sincere but troubled seekers of
God. They had never heard that Christ's death secured for
them a *permanent* and *total* forgiveness and righteous standing with God apart from works — that they could come to
God by faith in Christ alone.

JUSTIFICATION BY FAITH:
A NEGLECTED DOCTRINE

Down through the dark history of the church, this fact
of "justification by faith" has been the most maligned, misunderstood, and neglected truth of the Christian faith. A failure
to properly understand and accept the reality of having been

declared irrevocably righteous by God has stripped believers of the assurance of their standing with God and has crippled them into thinking they must be on an endless treadmill of works in order to maintain their acceptance with God.

It's hard to see how this vital truth could be missed by anyone who's seeking to carefully examine and teach the Word, since it's the heart of the message of the gospel. What Jesus had introduced in numerous parables in the Gospels concerning justification, Paul explained doctrinally in the Epistles, particularly in Romans and Galatians.

Obviously the reason Paul made such an emphasis upon this truth is because of the impact this doctrine had upon his own life. He makes this clear in his word of caution to the Philippians. In that letter to this young church, Paul seeks to undo some of the erroneous teaching that a group of super-religious Pharisaical Jews had sown behind his back and which subtly contradicted his previous teaching.

These Judaizers were Jews who in some ways accepted Jesus as the Messiah, but believed it was still imperative to keep all the old Mosaic laws, as well as being circumcised, if man was to be accepted by God. This was diametrically opposed to what Paul had taught. His emphasis was upon faith alone as being sufficient to bring about salvation.

In his admonishment to the church in Philippians 3:1-9, Paul argues that the truly circumcised person is the one who worships God in the Spirit and puts no confidence in fleshly rituals or deeds. He then cites his own admirable testimony of how blameless he was in his keeping of the Jewish laws and his zealous persecution of the church, prior to his conversion.

Here's what he says: **"If anyone else has a mind to put confidence in the flesh, I far more: circumcised the**

eighth day, of the nation of Israel, of the tribe of Benjamin, a Hebrew of Hebrews; as to the Law, a Pharisee; as to zeal, a persecutor of the church..."

Now, notice what he says about his "law-keeping": **"...as to the righteousness which is in the Law, *found blameless"* (Philippians 3:4b-6).

TWO KINDS OF RIGHTEOUSNESS

You can see from what Paul just said that there are *two* kinds of righteousness. We've already discussed the first one, that which belongs exclusively to Christ and is imputed or credited to the one who does nothing more than place faith in Christ's atoning death. But the second kind of righteousness is that which comes out of an attempt to keep God's Law. This is strictly relative. In other words, God's perfect righteousness might be looked at as a standard representing 100 percent. All human efforts to keep God's laws measure somewhere from zero to one hundred, with *no one* reaching 100 percent.

As men look at our law-keeping, they applaud enthusiastically the closer we get to 100 percent, and usually we pat ourselves on the back. But from God's perspective, *anything* less than 100 percent perfect law-keeping flunks. That's what Isaiah meant when he said, **"All *our* righteousnesses are as filthy rags"** in God's sight (Isaiah 64:6).

You've heard the saying, "The enemy of the best is the good." Nowhere is that more true than in this matter of righteousness. Although Paul could brag more than any Pharisee about how righteous he was in relation to keeping the Mosaic law, look at his own estimation of his righteousness as over against that which he received from Christ. He says, **"I count all things** *[all those humanly produced good deeds]* **to be** *loss* **in view of the surpassing value of knowing Christ Jesus my Lord, for whom I have suffered the loss of all things, and count them but rubbish in order that I may gain Christ, and may be found in Him,** *not having a righteousness of my own derived from the Law, but that which is through faith in Christ, the righteousness which comes from God on the basis of faith"* (Philippians 3:8, 9).

Paul's whole point is that his efforts to attain a righteousness God could accept exceeded everyone else's efforts. Yet all this effort did not save him. Paul concludes that if his righteousness didn't save him, then no one else's lawkeeping would save them either.

ISRAEL, GOD'S GREAT HISTORICAL LESSON

Paul explains why the majority of the nation of Israel stubbornly clung to the wrong kind of righteousness and thereby missed out on God's salvation. **"But Israel, pursuing a law of righteousness, did not arrive at that law. Why? Because they did not pursue it by** *faith,* **but as though it were by** *works.* **They stumbled over** *the stumbling stone [Jesus]"* (Romans 9:31-32).

Then Paul gives an even more devastating revelation, **"For I bear them witness that they have a zeal for God, but not in accordance with knowledge. For not knowing about God's righteousness, and seeking to establish their own, they did not subject themselves to the righteousness of God. For Christ is the end of the law for righteousness to everyone who believes"** (Romans 10:2-4).

Paul wasn't just picking on his fellow Jews here. His

heart's desire and constant prayer to God were for their eyes
to be opened to see — that they might see their mistake of
rejecting God's way to be made righteous and instead trusting
in their own righteousness.

I'M JUSTIFIED—SO WHAT?

I've used a lot of pages so far in this chapter to say
two things over and over.

First, on the basis of Christ's propitiatory work on
the cross, God's offended character has been satisfied and
God is now free to impart a new dimension to all who receive
His Son as Savior. This new dimension is twofold. He both
clothes the person who believes in Him with His righteousness, and He declares them judicially righteous. The first act
is called "imputed righteousness," and the second is called
"justification."

He sees me through the grid of Jesus' righteousness,
and therefore I am as acceptable to Him as His Son Jesus is,
regardless of my daily performance.

The second point I've stressed is that this righteousness is given to a person, free and complete, the moment he
places faith in Christ as Savior. It can not be improved upon,
added to, nor ever revoked. The declaration of righteousness
is a divine fiat that God Himself cannot revoke.

God assures us that He would not revoke our justification even if He could, **"What, then, shall we say in
response to this? If God is for us, who can be against us?
He who did not spare his own Son, but gave him up for us
all — how will he not also, along with him, graciously give
us all things? Who will bring any charge against those
whom God has chosen? It is God who justifies"** (Romans
8:31-33 NIV).

The ramifications in the life of the believer of "justifi-cation by faith" are incredible. We'll focus on the three major benefits: peace with God, a standing in grace, and no more condemnation.

PEACE WITH GOD

The Apostle Paul concluded, **"Therefore having been justified by faith, we have *peace with God* through our Lord Jesus Christ"** (Romans 5:1).

"Having been justified" is in the aorist verb tense in the original Greek. This means it happened at a point of time in the past, and the implication here is that it never need be repeated because its effects go on forever.

It's imperative that once and for all we get straight in our minds the fact that we *have been* justified. If we don't, it's impossible to experience "peace with God." If we think our relationship with God is in constant jeopardy because of our failure to live the Christian life correctly, then we will be a nervous wreck. We will be constantly worrying whether God is going to disown us because our performance wasn't good enough. I can never experience peace with God until I begin to count as true the fact that I have been given Christ's righteousness and my eternal relationship with God is secure.

In their book, *Guilt and Freedom,*[1] Bruce Narramore and Bill Counts point out the hidden dangers of not seeing ourselves as God sees us. They correctly show that sin erect-ed very real barriers between God and man, and that although Christ has torn down the barriers and enabled God to recon-cile men to Himself, there remain psychological barriers on the part of man. Man's knowledge of his failure to please God has brought fear of punishment, fear of rejection, and a loss of self-esteem.

There is absolutely no way to have these psychological barriers removed until we accept as true the fact that God is now at peace with us because He has justified us once and for all. If I'm the least bit fuzzy in my thinking about this, then in spite of myself, I'm going to live with fear of punishment and rejection by God each time I fail Him. Eventually my sense of guilt will pile so high that I will see myself as of absolutely no worth to God.

Maybe you've never thought of it this way, but to have those kind of feelings about yourself is like a slap in the face to Jesus. In essence, what we are saying is that we have higher standards for ourselves than God does. This whole line of thinking is both conceited and false. God is satisfied with what Christ did for us; why can't we be?

If God says He is at peace with *us* on the basis of our justification, then what right do we have not to be at peace with God?

PEACE WITH OURSELVES AND OTHERS

One thing is certain, if we don't have peace with God, then it will be impossible to be at peace with ourselves. We will be constantly condemning ourselves for our failures. Self-condemnation keeps us focused inward instead of on Jesus and all He did to remove God's wrath from us.

It is also impossible to be at peace with others if you haven't first settled in your mind that God is at peace with you. The last great commandment Jesus gave to His disciples was **"Love one another, even** [in the same way] **as I have loved you"** (John 13:34). If you're not convinced that God's love for you is unconditional on the basis of His justification of you, then your love for others won't be unconditional either. You will accept them in the same way you believe you are accepted by God.

That's the way you'll respond to those around you. When they meet your expectations, you'll give them unconditional acceptance. When they let you down, you'll withdraw your full acceptance of them until they shape up and start performing up to your standards again.

All this fouled-up thinking is straightened out by simply believing that what God says is true of us, is really true. We *have been* justified, and now God is at peace with us and nothing will ever cause Him to stop being at peace with us.

The only issue is, will we believe what He says about our justification and be at peace with him?

A STANDING IN AMAZING GRACE

A second great benefit which has come to the believer through justification by faith is a new standing in grace.

"Therefore having been justified by faith, we have peace with God through our Lord Jesus Christ, through whom also we have obtained our introduction by faith into this *grace in which we stand*" (Romans 5;1,2).

Remember that we defined grace as being "all that God has set Himself free to do for us on the basis of the cross completely apart from any human merit." If we can earn it in any way, then it can't be given to us on the basis of grace.

Paul tells us in this passage in Romans that we have a standing in grace. This means God cannot deal with us in any other way than grace — that is our new standing with Him. There'll never be a time in our lives when God will require us to deserve or earn any blessing or favor from Him. God tells us, **"As you have therefore received Christ Jesus the Lord,** so [continue to] **walk in Him"** (Colossians 2:6 NKJV). We received the Lord by grace through faith. We are to live moment by moment by grace through faith.

I don't know why it's so hard for people to really believe this. Most can accept the fact that they could do nothing to deserve or earn their initial salvation. But most Christians have gotten the idea that they must earn the right to be used by God or receive His blessings after becoming His child.

I found myself subtly slipping into this thinking only recently. I was given a cruise to Mexico. It was like a dream come true. I was waited on hand and foot. The food was sensational. There were no telephones ringing or appointments to keep. But about the third day out, I began to feel guilty about having such a great time. I was feeling guilty because I felt I didn't really deserve such a display of God's love.

Then the Lord reminded me, "When did you *ever* deserve any of My blessings?"

That is really the truth! When did any of us ever deserve anything from a holy and righteous God except His wrath? And yet, because He has declared us as righteous as His Son, Jesus, God is able to give us His gracious blessings at any time, quite apart from any merit in us. It's because of our standing in grace with Him.

THOU SHALT NOT SWEAT IT

One of the marvelous things about being in an atmosphere of grace is that you don't have to walk around on eggshells worrying about offending someone. I'm sure we've all known people who create anything but an atmosphere of grace. The whole time we are around them we feel we must watch our Ps and Qs. This kind of relationship gets to be a drag, and we soon don't want to be around a person like that.

This often becomes one of the major factors in marital problems. One of the partners has the other on such a performance-based relationship that if the other one doesn't always come across as the model mate, they really let them know that they've been displeased. Instead of freeing the offensive partner to become the ideal mate, it simply tightens him up worrying about whether he's just done something wrong or not. It definitely *isn't* an atmosphere of grace.

But with God we don't have to walk around on eggshells because we have a standing in grace with Him, and He just doesn't get bugged with us when we fail to perform the way He might want. You see, our acceptance with Him is based on one key factor only: we are in His Son and His Son's righteousness is in us.

That's what it means to be **"accepted in the beloved"** (Ephesians 1:6 KJV). Jesus is the Beloved, and since I'm in Him, and He's in me, I'm accepted by the Father in the same way He is.

NO MORE CONDEMNATION

The third, and yet perhaps least understood, benefit of justification is that God doesn't condemn us anymore. That's what Paul was talking about when he wrote, **"There is therefore now no condemnation for those who are in Christ Jesus"** (Romans 8:1).

Boy, do I ever remember the day that truth hit me! It exploded in my life like a bombshell. I was under such a pile of self-condemnation, and what I thought was God's condemnation, that I could hardly see out from under the pile.

I was reading that verse one day, and all of a sudden I discovered the word "now." I don't know where it had been all that time, but I saw it for the first time and did it ever speak to me! I realized right then that on the basis of everything Paul had said in the first seven chapters of Romans about Jesus' death and resurrection, I wasn't under God's condemnation now and never could be again. That set the stage for me to stop condemning myself and stop believing others who tried to make me feel guilty because I wasn't living up to their ideas of what a Christian ought to be.

The sheer magnitude of this "no condemnation" concept has obviously been hard for the Church to handle all down through its history. You can't find much written about it in early Church writings because it wasn't clearly taught or understood. Part of that reason has to do with an incorrect addition to the text of Romans 8:1. Let's take a look at it.

THE NAKED TRUTH OF "NO CONDEMNATION"

In the first verse of Romans 8, where Paul makes the summary statement that **"there is therefore now no condemnation for those who are in Christ Jesus,"** you'll notice that the King James Version of the Bible adds a further statement, **"...who walk not after the flesh, but after the Spirit."** This phrase is not in any of the earliest Greek manuscripts dating before the fourth century. It was obviously added by someone or a group of people sometime during the middle centuries of the Church. None of the most recent Bible translations include it.

It has been thought that the addition of this seemingly innocent and supposedly correct statement was the mistake of some scribe who glanced at the end of Romans 8:4, where this same phrase ends the verse, and accidentally copied it onto verse one.

I personally don't see how that could have happened, because it's inconceivable to me that any one man could have had such unsupervised liberty in copying the most sacred document in the possession of the church.

My personal opinion is that the naked truth of the statement that Paul made — "there is therefore now *no condemnation* for those who are in Christ Jesus" — was simply more than some of the early church fathers could handle. They were willing to grant that if we walked in the Spirit we couldn't be condemned, but they couldn't accept the fact that just being in Christ and His righteousness being in us could make us free of all condemnation.

But, praise God, that's exactly what Paul meant to say because that's the truth!

If we'll just accept the statement for what it says and not bring our own religious bias to it, we can soon discover that Paul had good grounds on which to tell us that there's no more condemnation for us.

But before we look at those grounds, we need to define just what it means to no longer be condemned.

CONDEMNED BY WHOM AND FOR WHAT?

There are two facets to the concept of "condemnation." First, there's the genuine reality of the fact that unless a person believes in the redemptive work of Christ on the cross, he *is* condemned to an eternal separation from God in a very real place called Hell.

But once that person has believed in Christ's substitutionary death in his place, Jesus Himself promised, **"Truly,**

truly, I say to you, he who hears My word, and believes Him who sent Me, has eternal life, and *does not come into condemnation,* but has passed out of death into life" (John 5:24).

So the issue of *eternal* condemnation is a settled matter in the life of a true believer in Jesus. That's the very essence of what Jesus was saying. If we've passed from death into life, we can't go back into death again unless God undid His whole work of justification, and there's no chance of that happening.

However, what's at stake in the misunderstanding of Romans 8:1 is whether, having been delivered from *eternal* condemnation, a believer can come back under any form of condemnation by God because of his behavior.

The answer to that is an absolute NO!

The very reason that verse is located where it is, is meant to establish the finality of the fact that we can never again be condemned by God from the minute we believe in Jesus as Savior. In Romans 7 we see the picture of the believer, Paul, going through the most despairing period of his Christian life. It seems to Paul like everything is condemning him — the Law of God, his own conscience, and possibly, even God Himself.

But one chapter later in Romans 8, Paul is joyously writing of the fact that **"If God be for us, who can be against us"** (verse 31 KJV). This is no longer a defeated and despairing believer.

Now, what do you think it was that brought him out of the despair of Romans 7 and into the victory of Romans 8?

One great fact!

He realized there was no more condemnation from the Law, from God, and consequently no legitimate condemnation from his own conscience, because he was *in* Christ Jesus. And the realization of that set him free to begin to allow the indwelling Holy Spirit to make him holy in his daily living and to actually live in, and out through him, the very righteousness of Christ.

Realizing that he didn't have to live *for* God in order not to be condemned, he began to relax and trust the Holy Spirit to live the Christian life *through* him. That's what he meant when he said God rejected the method of using laws to try to make people behave the right way, because it never worked (Romans 8:3). But the same result of righteousness was achieved by walking in dependence upon the indwelling Holy Spirit and letting Him produce the righteousness of God *in* him (Romans 8:4).

THE GROUNDS OF "NO CONDEMNATION"

Now let's look at just a couple of the arguments Paul calls upon to substantiate the fact that God will *never* condemn any of His children.

The first argument has a basis in the laws of jurisprudence which govern the courtrooms of America and other countries as well. There's a law called "the Law of Double Jeopardy." This law states that an individual cannot be subjected to a second trial and penalty for the same offense.

This has a perfect application in the case of God against man. God has already condemned Jesus *in our place* for every sin we will ever commit. For that reason, and true to the law of double jeopardy, He cannot and will not condemn the one who believes in Jesus as his substitute and Savior. One person has already taken our penalty. Now we don't have to.

Peter explains Jesus' taking our place in this way: **"For Christ also died for sins once for all, the *just for the unjust,* in order that He might bring us to God"** (1 Peter 3:18a). He was the **"just"** One and we were the **"unjust."**

GOD IS ON OUR SIDE

Paul's second argument as to why we can never be condemned by God, once we become His children, reaches deep into the very character of God Himself. Two attributes of God's character, His sovereignty and His immutability (unchangeableness), are called upon to witness to the fact that God is unalterably "for us" and could never condemn us again.

In Romans 8:31-35 Paul sums up this second argument by posing five penetrating questions, the answers of which form a powerful argument for God never again condemning us and why neither we nor anyone else can legitimately condemn us either.

The first question: "If God is for us, who is against us?" (verse 31). The very nature of the question implies that "whoever" might be against us, they don't amount to anything because the Almighty, Sovereign God of the Universe is for us.

This fact can be very comforting when you have made your stand for the Lord in a hostile situation and you feel a little like the Lone Ranger. Joshua, the prophet of old, quoted God, **"Have I not commanded you? Be strong and courageous! Do not tremble or be dismayed, for the Lord your God is with you wherever you go"** (Joshua 1:9).

The second question: "He who did not spare His own Son, but delivered Him up for us all, how will He not also with Him freely give us all things?" (Romans 8:32). The point here is that if, when we were still enemies of God, He gave up the most precious thing He had in our behalf, now that we're His children, will He give us less? Of course not!

The **"all things"** He's promised to freely give us refer to the thousands of privileges and blessings outlined in the promises of God throughout the entire Bible. They're like a treasure storehouse just waiting to be entered.

You can see, on the basis of this unequivocal statement, that there's no need to beg at the back door of heaven for any of your needs. Paul wrote to the Philippians, **"My God shall supply all your needs according to His riches in glory in Christ Jesus"** (Philippians 4:19).

Part of the blessing of knowing we can never be condemned again is the certainty that when we go to the Lord in prayer, we will find a gracious and loving acceptance no matter how we have been behaving in our Christian lives. You see, when we were His bitter enemies, He did the most for us, and He won't do less now that we're His children.

The third question: "Who will [is qualified to] **bring a charge against God's elect?"** (Romans 8:33). Who has a right to bring accusations or condemnations against a person who has been declared righteous by the sovereign Judge of the universe? The answer is, "Only the Judge Himself!" But will the Almighty Judge of Heaven do this? Paul doesn't even bother to answer the question with a No because the answer is so obvious. God is the One who at great cost justified man, so He's not about to declare man unjust and condemned again.

What it boils down to is that God can't reverse a sovereign, immutable declaration which He's already made, even if He wanted to. And since it cost God the most incredible price that He could pay to justify man, why would He now want to throw all that out and say it was all for nothing? There's no remote chance that He would. The cost was too great!

The fourth question: "Who was the one who condemns?" (Romans 8:34). There's a saying, "Don't count your critics: weigh them!" That really applies here. There may be ever so many people, including yourself, who will condemn you, but there's only One who has the *right* to, and that's Jesus Himself.

John tells us, **"For not even the Father judges any one, but He has given all judgment to the Son, in order that all may honor the Son, even as they honor the Father"** (John 5:22,23).

Now, the question is, will Jesus condemn the one whom the Father has already declared righteous? We must again answer with a resounding NO! To do so would contradict four of His mightiest works in our behalf.

The *first* was that **"He died for us."** The *second*, **"He was raised from the dead"** to prove the Father's acceptance of His atonement for us. *Third,* **"He sits at God's right hand"** as a glorified man assuring the fact that we'll also be there one day. The *fourth,* He is continually **"interceding for us"** as our high priest, which is the opposite of condemning us. (See Romans 8:34.)

The fifth question: "Who shall separate us from the love of Christ?" (Romans 8:35). Christ's love drove

Him to die for us when we were helpless, ungodly and enemies. His same love is the source of our security now that we
are in union with His very person. God's unchangeable love
flows even more toward His children.

Now, that's not to say there won't be those who *will*
condemn us and accuse us of having "fallen from God's
grace" because of some behavior which they've judged as
being unforgiveable. But nothing, not even wrong behavior,
can ever cause God to condemn one of His children again.
God will discipline us in grace, but He will never disown us.

Because so few believers really understand the depths
of this truth, they mistake the condemnation of Satan, fellow
believers, and their own consciences as being from God.
Satan is called "the accuser of the Brethren" in Revelation
12:10. He accuses believers because he knows it is futile to
accuse us before God. But if we are not anchored in the
bedrock truths of justification and imputed righteousness, we
will fall for Satan's accusations — actually thinking they're
from God.

SINCE GOD NO LONGER CONDEMNS, DO YOU?

Since God has gone to such great lengths to prove He
doesn't condemn us anymore, then do we have a right to condemn ourselves? No one can have a bold faith when he's
walking around condemning himself for his miserable performance as a child of God.

True faith comes from focusing on Christ and what
He's done for you through justification. But if you don't concentrate on that and instead focus on your behavior as a
believer, you'll soon end up being discouraged and condemning yourself for your failure to live up to what you know God
requires of you.

It's also true that if you condemn yourself for a shabby Christian life, you're bound to also have a critical view of others. We hate most in others what we hate about ourselves. Yet if Christ doesn't condemn a brother, but accepts Him on the basis of having declared him righteous in Christ, then what right do I have to condemn him? As the Scriptures say, **"Who are you to judge the servant of another? To his own master he stands or falls; and stand he will, for the Lord is able to make him stand"** (Romans 14:4).

What an incredible promise! Don't we all know some Christian friend who hasn't been living very close to God and we've taken all kinds of "spiritual" potshots at him? This verse of Scripture should give great encouragement to us because it says he is God's servant and the Lord is able to make him stand. And stand he will!

It may be that *our* condemnation of him is the very thing keeping him from seeing that God is not condemning him for having strayed. Nobody wants to snuggle up to a porcupine, and if an erring believer thinks God is still angry with him and just waiting to condemn him, he'll never want to come back into fellowship with the Lord.

Our loving and accepting attitude may be his path back.

JUSTIFICATION IS THE NAME OF THE GAME

I realize that this chapter has been the longest one in the book, but how could I have hurried through this most critical truth of justification by faith? If we aren't straight in our thinking on this subject, nothing else will work right in our Christian lives.

In summing it up, let me just say that justification is the work of God whereby He declares righteous, on the basis of faith alone, that one who simply believes in Jesus as Savior. This righteousness is something which is added to the believer when he believes and can never be taken away. It assures him of three great realities: peace with God, a standing in grace, and no more condemnation. And that's AMAZING GRACE!

CHAPTER 15

FORGIVENESS

Not long ago I was speaking to a group of young married couples about the truth of the total forgiveness in Jesus Christ. A young woman stayed around until everyone else had gone and then walked up and said, "I have a question."

"All right," I said. "How can I to help?"

She told me she and her husband were both believers, but they'd only been married about three months and were already having problems.

"I know this may sound stupid," she said, "but I can't forgive him because of something he did. And it was really as much my fault, I guess, as it was his."

She went on to tell me that they had sex together before they were married at his insistence. And now, every time he wanted to make love, she really resented him and couldn't forgive him for taking away her virginity before marriage.

The guilt on her face was apparent. And to make matters worse, her husband was sitting at the back of the room, waiting for us to finish talking. I had no idea what his attitude was about our conversation.

"I've got some great news for you," I began. "Do you know what Christ did with sin when He died for us?" I asked.

"Yes, He forgave it," she replied.

"How much of it?" I asked.

"Everything."

"How many of yours and your husband's sins did Jesus forgive?" I said.

"All of them," she answered.

"Well then," I said, "if God has forgiven you and your husband, don't you think you should forgive yourself and him too?"

"I'd never really thought about it that way before," she said. "Praise the Lord, I really *do* forgive him."

She thanked me and was about to turn around and head over to where her husband was waiting.

"I hate to hold you up," I said. "But there's one more thing you ought to know.

The expression on her face looked as if she thought I was going to withdraw some of the good news I had told her.

"The other thing is that God has not only forgiven you two, but *He has forgotten it's ever happened!* Here is God's promise, **'Their sins and their lawless deeds I will remember no more'** (Hebrews 10:17). Not only has He forgiven you, but He chose not to remember the sin. Christ's death on the cross made that possible. Now, since God has forgotten all about it, you should forget it also. Okay?"

"Wow! Thank you," she said. "This is the best news I've ever heard."

She turned and literally ran to back of the room. She grabbed her husband and hugged him so hard it almost knocked him off his chair. Needless to say, their love for each other flourished. Misunderstanding God's forgiveness has wrecked many marriages. Unforgiveness produces a sense of estrangement and alienation that leads to all kinds of relationship problems.

REDEMPTION IS THE GROUND OF FORGIVENESS

Now, before anyone is tempted to protest that my counsel to her made a light thing out of sin, let's see just how extensive God's forgiveness for sin really is.

As you have already seen, forgiveness is one of the results of Christ's redemptive work on the cross. As we'll see in the next chapter, freedom is another. Man's debt of sin was canceled out by Christ's redemption, making it possible for God to totally forgive us all our sins. Then He purchased us out of the slave market of sin and gave us freedom.

In this chapter we concentrate on what it means to be forgiven by God.

In Colossians Paul sets forth the extent of God's forgiveness in the clearest possible way. He speaks here to the young believers in the church at Colossae: **"And when you were dead in your transgressions [sins] and the uncircumcision of your flesh, He made you alive together with Him, having forgiven us all our [sins]"** (Colossians 2:13).

Three things are emphasized here. *First,* God says we were all dead in our sins at one time. This is the state of all of us before we came to Christ. We learned this in the chapter on spiritual death.

Second, God has made us alive in Christ. This is a fantastic truth, and we'll look at it carefully in the chapter on regeneration.

Third — and this is the facet of this passage on which we want to concentrate — God has **"...forgiven us all our sins."** The verb **"having forgiven"** in Colossians 2:13 is in the aorist tense in the original, meaning it happened at a point of time in the past. In other words, once God dealt with sin at the cross, it was a closed case.

I want us to lock in on one particular phrase in this
verse, **"forgiven us *all* our sins."**

Have you ever stopped to consider how much "all"
really is? A lawyer friend of mine told me about a legal decision from a case in Pennsylvania, the word "all" was defined
this way: "All includes everything and excludes nothing."

ALL ISN'T ALWAYS ALL, TO ALL

But you know, in the mind of the average Christian,
when he reads the words "having forgiven us all our sins," he
thinks it refers to all the sins he committed *before* he accepted Jesus. I used to think this.

To illustrate this diagram represents my life:

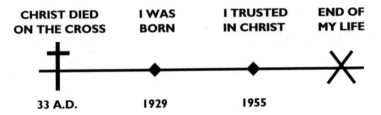

CHRIST DIED ON THE CROSS	I WAS BORN	I TRUSTED IN CHRIST	END OF MY LIFE
33 A.D.	1929	1955	

Up here to the left, Christ died for my sins in A.D. 33.
Further on in history, a guy named Hal Lindsey was born in
1929. Then in 1955, he accepted Jesus Christ.

Okay — born, 1929, received Christ, 1955. I used to
think that when I believed in Jesus Christ as my personal
Savior, He forgave me all my sins from the day I was born up
until 1955 on the basis of His death in A.D. 33. I don't know
what I thought His provision was for the rest of my life! I
guess I felt I had to somehow get forgiveness for all my
future sins by confessing each one right after I did it.

But how many of my sins were future when Christ

died? ALL OF THEM! Do you know that the sins I committed from 1955 until the day I go to be with Christ are just as much paid for as the previous ones? They were all so offensive to a holy God, that in A.D. 33 He *had* to deal with *everything* I would ever do wrong. In order for God to have forgiven me in 1955, He had to have forgiven me for all future sins *or He could not have accepted me in the first place!* You see, my future sins were as real and repugnant to God as my past ones. Remember God's omniscience.

HALF A CROSS ISN'T ENOUGH FOR SALVATION

Many people have a concept of a cross that only looks to the rear of their lives, but never looks ahead. That's only half of a cross and that's really no cross at all. When God says He forgave us all our sins, that's a cross with two arms, one stretching back into our past and one reaching into our future. Anything less than an all-inclusive forgiveness on the timeline of history falls pathetically short of God's infinite provision for sin.

THE TWO MOST IMPORTANT TRUTHS ABOUT FORGIVENESS

First, we saw in our chapter on redemption that when Christ went to the cross, He took our certificates of debt, which list *all* the sins of all mankind, and once and for all paid the penalty for them. This took sin out of the way as a barrier to God (Colossians 2:14).

Then, in Hebrews 10:14 and 17, another facet of this great truth is revealed. By Christ's offering of Himself as our sacrifice, He has provided a forgiveness for us that's *eternal* and *irreversible*. Verse 17 says, **"And their sins and their lawless deeds I will *remember* no more."**

Isaiah the prophet quoted the Lord as saying the same thing: **"I, even I, am the one who wipes out your transgressions for My own sake; and I will not *remember* your sins"** (Isaiah 43:25).

These two truths form the bedrock foundation upon which you must build in order to experience the reality of God's forgiveness in your daily life.

First, all your sins—past, present, and future—were forgiven when you believed in Jesus. There are none He hasn't already forgiven.

Second, not only has He forgiven you *all* your sins, but He's wiped them out from His own memory forever. They'll never be brought up against you again.

CAN WE FORGIVE AS GOD HAS?

If God has forgiven us all our sins and isn't holding them against us anymore, then what should our attitude be about sins in ourselves and others? Thousands of hospital beds, mental institutions, and jails are filled with people who have never forgiven themselves or others for wrongdoing. This kind of poison eats away at a person until real illness or damaging hostility results.

One of the key factors in unhappy marriages is that two people living in such intimate proximity see the worst side of each other. In this kind of emotionally charged relationship, while the rough edges are being refined, things are often said and done that are unkind or cruel. If these things are allowed to fester and are never forgiven, bitterness and resentment can build up inside the two partners resulting in complete estrangement.

More and more people take what they consider the easy "out" when this kind of alienation occurs — divorce. But this does not solve the real problem, which is the inability to forgive. All they do is take the problem into the next marriage. Usually the new partner gets punished with an even greater buildup of hostility.

In many cases, marriages that appear to be fairly normal on the outside also suffer because there's unforgiveness on the part of one or both partners. They punish each other by sexual neglect, sloppy housekeeping and personal grooming, failure to achieve in their jobs, attention to others of the opposite sex, fighting, frigidity, constant criticism and nagging, and on and on. Both they and their children suffer from the lack of forgiveness.

There are also many people who have never been able to forgive themselves for their past sins. Maybe they've had a secret habit which they've felt was sin, and because they can't forgive *themselves*, they develop a sense of shame that results in a terrible self-image. They feel they're no good, and they develop a self-consciousness and inferiority complex.

Or, a knowledge of their inner sin-life causes some people to develop a defensiveness that makes them hostile and argumentative. Their attitude is no matter how little they really think of themselves, they're going to be very sure no one gets close enough to see how raunchy they are inside. This is "the-best-defense-is-an-offense" philosophy.

IS ALL THIS BITTERNESS NECESSARY?

There's only one basis on which we can fully forgive ourselves and others for sins and shortcomings. We must remember and believe that God has already forgiven us for the sins that are causing the bitterness. If God has forgiven us and is not holding our sins against us, then we should not hold them against ourselves. If we do, it will only lead us into more sin because we will not be able to walk by faith. We cannot trust God if we think He is holding our past sins against us. Satan know this and goes all out to blind us to the full meaning of God's forgiveness.

Now, you might be thinking to yourself, "Yes, but if you only knew what he did to me, you would see why I can't forgive him."

But you know, God could say that to us about our sins too. They sent His beloved Son to the cross to suffer in a way that none of us could ever imagine. And yet, God has forgiven us, for Christ's sake.

For me to fail to forgive myself or anyone else who has offended me is to say that I have a higher standard of forgiveness than God. We must remember that God already has forgiven whatever it is I can't forgive. And He forgave me things that are infinitely more hurtful than what any mere human can do to me.

THE SIN SYNDROME: SIN, GUILT, ESTRANGEMENT

A failure to understand properly the full extent of God's forgiveness will always hamper our spiritual lives. Sin produces an inevitable cycle, even after we are God's children.

When we sin, the Holy Spirit convicts us and we experience a bonafide conviction which is referred to in 2 Corinthians 7:8-11 as **"godly sorrow."** However, if that "sorrow" is not properly related to God's forgiveness, it will lead to guilt and that will lead to estrangement from God. This estrangement doesn't mean we have lost our relationship with God. But it can cause us to live in fear of God's punishment or rejection. This leads to a sense of unworthiness that makes it impossible to believe God for His provisions for victory in daily living. Unbelief results in more defeat, which results in greater unbelief and greater defeat.

DEALING WITH GUILT, BOTH REAL AND FALSE

Now, how can the "sin syndrome" of sin, guilt, and estrangement be broken? We know we don't stop committing sins even though we're believers. The Spirit testifies, **"If we [believers] claim we have not sinned, we make him out to be a liar and his word has no place in our lives"** (1 John 1:10 NIV). So how can we keep from developing guilt which leads to estrangement from God?

Dealing With Real Guilt Here is the solution for real guilt. When I knowingly sin, It breaks my FELLOWSHIP WITH GOD, NOT MY ETERNAL RELATONSHIP. I must confess my sin to the Lord in order to remove hinderances to fellowship with Him, according to 1 John 1:9. The word "confess" is a combination of two Greek words, *homo* and *logeo* (ομολογεω). These two words together mean "to say the same thing about something that someone else says." In this case, when I've sinned, I must say the same thing about my sin that God says about it. In other words, I must agree verbally with God about my known sins.

Now, what does God say about my sin?

First, He says it *is* sin. So I agree with God that what

I just did was sin. I don't try to make excuses for myself or deny the sin. I fully own up to what I have done. Since I know that my sins have already been forgiven as far as my eternal relationship is concerned, I can be honest with God about my sin.

Second, God says He *has* forgiven all my sins, including this one I just committed. So I look to the cross of Jesus and there remind myself of the great fact of my forever forgiveness which He purchased there. Then I thank Him that in His sight my sin has *already been* forgiven. Jesus has already suffered and died for the penalty of that sin. I know that I do not have to beg God to apply a forgiveness that has already been given. All I must do is claim it.

Third, out of appreciation for such grace in forgiveness, I accept it gratefully, turn from my sin, and begin to focus consciously upon the Lord Jesus again, drawing upon the Holy Spirit, who is living in me and who alone can empower me not to sin.

Dealing With False Guilt After I have confessed a sin, Satan will attempt to accuse my conscience and make me believe that I am really not forgiven. He will cause me to feel, "God won't forgive me this time. I have just failed too often for Him to forgive me again. Surely I must do something to make God more disposed to forgive me." This sort of thinking is an insult to God's grace. It's bad enough that we have sinned in the first place. But it is even worse when we refuse to believe God's Word and become vulnerable to greater sin.

We deal with real guilt by confessing our sins to God and claiming His forgiveness. We deal with false guilt by believing God's promises about forgiveness. If we do not, the following deadly syndrome sets in.

THE CONSEQUENCES OF
NOT RELATING SIN TO THE CROSS

When a believer sins, he's immediately convicted by the Spirit. Even if he's hardened his heart by ignoring the Spirit's conviction many times before. Our Heavenly Father can always be counted on to get through to His erring child sooner or later. But if the believer doesn't immediately relate his sin to the cross and the forgiveness that's already his because of it, then it will lead to a sense of guilt which is not from God. And that guilt will lead into a temporal estrangement from God.

Now, when we sin, a strange phenomenon sets in. We instinctively know that someone has to pay. Even if we don't recognize this on the conscious level, it occurs in our subconscious minds.

Since we can't cope with this unresolved inner conviction, we'll handle it in one of three ways. Either we will punish ourselves in an effort to make up for the sin; or we'll punish someone else; or we will look to the cross of Jesus and believe that He has already been punished in our place, so that we have no need to punish ourselves or anyone else.

SIN IS NO LONGER THE ISSUE

What I've been trying to say through this whole chapter is that there's no longer any reason to focus on past sins. The work of Christ in redemption has so completely dealt with our sins that they can never again be brought up against us. This sets us free to focus on Christ's power to keep us from yielding to present temptation.

Now, you may wonder; if sin is no longer an issue with God, what should my attitude be toward sin when I fail?

As I already discussed, it should be confessed and God's forgiveness appropriated. But if we become insensitive to the Spirit's conviction about sin, and become careless about saying No to temptation and trusting the Holy Spirit to give us victory over it, God will discipline us. But His discipline is done in love, not anger (Hebrews 12:6).

The words "discipline" and "training" are interchangeable. God's discipline is always forward looking, and that's why it's comparable to training. The Lord does not *punish* the believer. That would be getting even for offending Him, and that has already been borne by Christ for us.

When God sees His child continually refuse to depend upon the Holy Spirit for deliverance from temptations, He will begin to train and discipline him. This is done so that the believer will come to depend upon Him in the future. God knows we are only happy when we are obedient to the inner prompting of His Spirit. He also knows that our new selves are slaves of righteousness, because our new natures always want to follow God. The born-again man will be miserable living in sin.

But even when God has to discipline us, His focus is not on our past sins but on avoiding sin in the future. God's goal is to get us to walk moment by moment in a faith dependence on His indwelling Spirit.

I know it worries some people to hear that our sins are no longer the big issue with God. These people usually wonder what will motivate people to keep in line if they aren't scared stiff of what God is going to do to them if they sin. Being afraid of God does not keep a person from sinning. I have sinned while trembling with fear of what God was going to do to me.

The greatest motive for living a righteous life is thanksgiving for all that God has done to save us which

results in true love for Him. This book will help you understand this. And the Bible says the only means of living a victorious life is FAITH, NOT FEAR. **"This is *love* for God: to
obey his commands. And his commands are not burden-
some, for everyone born of God overcomes the world.
This is the victory that has overcome the world, even our
faith. Who is it that overcomes the world? Only he who
believes that Jesus is the Son of God"** (1 John 5:3-5 NIV).

I can't find a verse of Scripture that teaches a believer
to avoid sins by "worrying about them" as a proper motivation for serving God. But there are abundant verses that teach
us that God isn't alienated from us anymore, now that we are
His children. All He requires of us is to walk by faith so we
won't fulfill the lusts of our sinful natures. **"So I say, live by
the Spirit, and you will not gratify the desires of the sinful
nature"** and **"We live by faith, not by sight"** (Galatians 5:16
and 2 Corinthians 5:7 NIV).

It's easy to walk by faith when you *know* you're forgiven. You're not afraid to be honest with God if you *know*
He isn't just waiting for you to sin so He can get even with
you. You can't wait to love and serve a God whose *only* attitude toward you is one of love and complete acceptance.

Isn't it great to know you're forgiven?

Now, let the realization of this cause you to forgive
yourself for that thing which you've been holding in your
conscience. And let it also lead you to forgive those toward
whom you've been harboring bitterness and unforgiveness.
**"And be kind to one another, tender-hearted, *forgiving*
each other, just as God in Christ also *has forgiven* you"**
(Ephesians 4:32).

This is the pathway to real freedom!

CHAPTER 16

FREEDOM

When we've been there ten thousand years,
Bright shining as the sun,
We've no less days to sing God's praise,
Than when we'd first begun.

— JOHN NEWTON

If there's one word that expresses the yearning of mankind today, it is FREEDOM.

In every corner of our world there is a cry for freedom. We have seen it in the collapse of the former Soviet empire, in the collapse of the Iron Curtain and the freeing of Eastern Europe, in the end of apartheid in South Africa and in the growing demands for human rights from Mongolia to the Middle East.

In every language created by man, "freedom" is a word that has always been cherished. Regardless of what a person owns, they would rather lose their possessions to a flood or a fire than to lose their freedom.

A quick summary of any world history text will reveal the extent to which man has been held in bondage. Slavery has been a force of civilization from the days before known history. It still exists in some parts of Africa, Asia, and Latin America.

What we are learning, however, is that a person does not need to be restrained in iron shackles to be a slave. Millions are held captive in their mind and spirit by forces that seem to be beyond their control.

SLAVERY HAS MANY FACES

You don't have to have irons around your legs to be a slave. The crowd to whom Jesus said, **"If therefore the Son**

shall make you free, you shall be free indeed" (John 8:36), were not standing there in shackles. In fact, they were the ruling elite of the nation of Israel. Their response to this straightforward rebuke showed how little they realized their true condition: **"We are Abraham's offspring, and have never yet been enslaved to any one; how is it that You say, 'You shall become free'?"** (John 8:33).

Jesus went on to explain to them that their bondage was an inner one. They belonged to Satan.

In chapter five we saw that one of the barriers separating God and man was man's slavery to Satan. But man was also a slave to two other forces, the old sin nature and the Law, and he just as desperately needed to be set free from them as from Satan himself.

This chapter shows how the redemptive work of Christ on the cross unshackled mankind and allowed God to give us freedom from (1) the tyranny of our inborn sin natures, (2) the principle of law with its demands for obedience or death, and (3) that vicious slave master of men, Satan.

TWENTIETH-CENTURY ALLEGORY

In the first few verses of Romans 7, there is a story that opened my understanding to how I have been set free from my sin nature, from bondage to the Law, and from the Evil One.

Let me take the liberty to paraphrase Paul's example.

There was once a charming, lovely and gentle woman who was married to a harsh and demanding perfectionist. All he did, from the day they were married, was give her rules of how he expected her to behave as his wife. Nothing was ever good enough for him. No matter how hard she tried to please him, she always broke some of his rules. He placed more and more demands on her and never once offered to help.

Years went by and things kept going from bad to worse. She spent most of her time worrying about whether she had upset him, and alternately feeling guilty for her failures, then hostile and resentful. She finally began to live on the edge of despair.

Now, I don't mean to give the impression that this husband was not a moral man. He was known for being just and moral. As far as scruples, honesty and honor were concerned, he was perfect. But he was rigid, cold, insensitive and without compassion. He seemed to feel that if he showed mercy, it would compromise his sense of duty and justice.

Well, not being able to live with the sense of failure that was now a daily part of her life, she began to wish secretly that somehow he would leave her. She felt guilty about it, but she wished he would die. But, alas, he was in perfect health and so very moral that divorce was entirely out of the question.

Just when things became unbearable, she met another man. And what a man he was! He was everything her husband was in the way of honor and morality, but was beautifully combined with gentleness, compassion and sensitivity. It shocked her to realize that this man was everything she had ever dreamed of.

This new man could see how desperately unhappy she was because of the terrible demands her husband kept putting on her. He could also see that he did not love her or take care of her real emotional needs.

They both fell deeply in love with each other. But because he was honorable, he knew he had to do things lawfully. So he came to her with a plan. Since her husband would not leave her or die, thus breaking her relationship to him, the only other solution would be for her to die. Then there would be a legal severance of relationship, and she would be free to marry the him.

Viola! What an ingenious plan. There's only one little problem. If she is dead, she cannot marry him either.

You're way ahead of me, right? She would have to be raised from the dead and become alive again. Because our new husband was willing to die for us first, He became the first to be resurrected into eternal life. And that made it possible for Him to raise us into His new life with Him. And then, in the truest sense of marriage, He caused us to become inseparably united with Him, "For we are members of His body, of His flesh and of His bones" (Ephesians 5:30 NKJV).

God's Word also reveals about this, **"For if we have become united with Him in the likeness of His *death*, certainly we shall be also in the likeness of His *resurrection*... Now if we have *died* with Christ, we believe that we shall also *live* with Him... Even so consider yourselves to be *dead* to sin, but *alive* to God in Christ Jesus"** (Romans 6:5, 8,11).

God put all of us into an intimate, inseparable union with His Son at the moment of salvation through the miracle of the Baptism of the Holy Spirit, **"For by one Spirit we were all baptized into one body—whether Jews or Greeks, whether slaves or free—and have all been made to drink into one Spirit"** (1 Corinthians 12:13 NKJV).

THE CHARACTERS OF THE ALLEGORY

I'm sure by now you've pretty well figured out who the characters are in this allegory. You, the believer, are the *wife*. The tyrannical, perfectionist *husband* is the Law of God. The *new husband* is the Lord Jesus Christ.

This demanding husband would not die. So God's solution was to crucify us through union with Jesus, thus legally breaking the Law's authority over us. Through this same union with Christ, He raised us into the Christ's new resurrection life where the Law can never have claim on us again.

OUR DEATH UNDER THE LAW

The Law said "keep me or die." We could not keep it, so we died under its penalty. Now, in our new life, it can never have jurisdiction over us again. As the Holy Spirit testified through Paul, **"For through the Law I died to the Law, that I might live to God. I have been crucified with Christ; and it is no longer I who live, but Christ lives in me; and the life which I now live in the flesh I live by faith in the Son of God, who loved me, and delivered Himself up for me"** (Galatians 2:19-20).

OUR DEATH BROKE SATAN
AND THE SIN NATURE AUTHORITY ALSO

On the basis of this same transaction, the authority of *Satan* and the *sin nature* over us has also been broken. Legally they have no more authority over us. They have no right to touch us unless we foolishly give it to them.

JUST WHAT IS IT THAT'S DEAD?

It's extremely important to get straight in our minds just what or who it is that's dead. I've seen people going around trying to crucify themselves and thereby trying to get rid of the power of sin and Satan. But Paul says in Romans 6:6 (paraphrased), **". . . that our old self was crucified with Christ, for the purpose that our body of sin** [our body still has the sin nature in it] **might be rendered powerless, so that we should no longer be slaves to the sin nature."**

Your **"old self"** is all that you were — with your appetites, drives, desires, habits, self-centeredness, and rebellion toward God — *before* you believed in Jesus and were given a "new self." At the moment you received Christ, your "old self," sometimes called the "old man," was judicially declared to be dead. Its right to dominate you was broken.

But there's nothing so great about being dead. Being "alive" is where the action is! And that's why Jesus raised us up with Him from the dead into a whole new realm of life. This "new self," with its resurrection kind of life, can no longer be legally dominated by any of those powers which had so easily dominated the "old man."

Now, when we were raised with Christ into this new dimension of life, our "old self" was left behind in the grave. The three times it's referred to in the Bible, it's spoken of as legally dead. In Romans 6:6 it specifically says that **"our old self *was crucified* with Christ."** (See also Ephesians 4:22-24; Colossians 3:9,10.)

So, as far as I can see, the only enemy we have that is legally dead is the "old self" or "old man." All the other foes dedicated to our destruction are still very much alive. But the whole basis of our freedom over them is that we have died in our relationship to them. The authority of these adversaries — the *sin nature*, the *Law*, and *Satan* — has forever been broken so that we do not have to be under their power again. We are now free to send our new Husband to deal with them when they come to the door and try to entice us.

FREEDOM FROM THE *POWER*
AS WELL AS THE *PENALTY*

There are *two* aspects to the freedom which the
redemptive work of Christ has made available to men. First,
we've been set free from the *penalty* of sin by the death of
Christ *for* us (1 Corinthians 15:3). That took care of removing the barriers that separated us from a holy and righteous
God.

But second, His death also has provided for a daily
deliverance of believers from the *power* of sin. To make this
possible, Christ died, not only *for* sins, but for the *sinner himself* (Romans 6:10). This made it possible for the Holy Spirit
on a righteous basis to take up permanent residence in every
believer — even though he still has the sin nature dwelling in
his body as long as he lives.

Paul tells us this is the reason we can now **"consider
ourselves to be dead to** [the sin nature]**, but alive to God in
Christ Jesus"** (Romans 6:11).

A CLOSER LOOK AT OUR FREEDOM

Let us consider in more depth the extent of the freedom from the sin nature, the principle of law, and Satan's
authority Christ's redemption has made possible.

To understand fully the far-reaching implications of
this new liberty, however, it must be kept in mind that at the
instant we believed in Christ, the *actual* and *legal* authority of
these three great enemies of the believer was judicially severed. But whether their control and power has, in fact, ceased
over us depends *entirely* upon whether we claim this victory
and by faith depend on the indwelling Holy Spirit to deal with
their attempts to illegally control us again.

For we must realize that these are vicious and adamant enemies who are relentless in their efforts to regain the dominion they had over us. As long as we live in this body they will constantly seek to entice us to submit to them again.

But God has made provision for all of our needs, and this case is no different. God never intended for *us* to deal with these three enemies in our own power.

So He sent the third person of the Godhead, the Holy Spirit, to take up permanent residence in our new spiritual nature. Now it is the job of the Holy Spirit to deal with the temptations of the old sin nature, the Law, and Satan. We will look at the work of the Holy Spirit in greater detail in the next chapter.

In chapter four I discussed in depth what the sin nature is and how it operates in man, so I only want to briefly review that here, and then look at the extent of our freedom from it.

THE OLD SIN NATURE

The old sin nature is that predisposition toward rebellion against God with which we are all born. It is the old sinful nature that we inherited from Adam. That's what Paul meant in Romans 5:12: **"Through one man sin** *[sin and its product, the sin nature]* **entered into the world."**

This nature is sometimes referred to as "sin" in the singular. That's the way Paul uses it in the principle passages of Scripture which teach about this sinful nature, Romans 6, 7, and 8. It is also called "the flesh." Occasionally "flesh" has a neutral or even holy meaning, but that is always evident by the immediate context.

In chapter four I used the science-fiction movie as an

illustration. Remember the extra-terrestrials that planted tiny receiving sets in the the brain of their human victims? Then they transmitted instructions from space to their robot-like victims who were programmed to obey.

That's much the way the old sin nature works in us. It's the "sin mechanism" inside us that is constantly being energized by signals from Satan. We are no longer the slaves of this "sin mechanism" because God has unplugged it. So don't plug it back in — get the point? In the next chapter we'll see more clearly what God has done to set us free from our spiritual enemies.

SATAN GETS AT US THROUGH THE LAW

One of the favorite tactics of Satan in trying to keep believers enslaved is to get them on the treadmill of trying to live for God by keeping all His Laws. In chapter eleven of my book, *Satan Is Alive and Well on Planet Earth*[1], I show what the Law is, how it works on man, and why it's completely impotent as an instrument for helping us live holy lives. I'm going to reemphasize some of that material here.

First, let us deal with what makes us sin in our daily lives as believers. Sometimes when we sin we like to say, "The Devil made me do it." There is usually a twinkle in our eye when we say it. It may help us get off the hook in our own minds, but Satan is not to blame for most of our sins.

There are two ingredients necessary for a person to sin. In Romans 7:5 Paul says, **"For while we were in the flesh** [before we became believers]**, the *sinful passions*, which were *aroused by the Law*, were at work in the members of our body to bear fruit for death."**

Here Paul indicates there are two things at work within a non-believer to make him sin: his sinful passions, or sin

nature as it's sometimes called, and the Law. When the Law
stirs up the sinful passions, rebellion against the Law occurs
and that's what the Bible calls "sin."

This principle of law works exactly the same way in
us after we become a child of God. Paul shared his own
experience as a young believer, **"I would not have come to
know sin except through the Law; for I would not have
known about coveting if the Law had not said, 'You shall
not covet.' But sin, taking opportunity through the commandment, produced in me coveting of every kind; for
apart from the Law sin is dead"** (Romans 7:7,8).

The secular field of psychology has noticed this same
tendency in man to do just the opposite of what he's commanded to do. They call it the "law of reverse psychology."
If you want someone to do something, tell him to do just the
opposite. Most parents have figured this out before their children get very old.

THE LAW IS NOT THE CULPRIT

I know that all this tends to put the law in a bad light,
whether God's law or man's law. But the law isn't the real
problem. Those sinful passions or sin natures that get stirred
up by the Law are the problem.

Now, you might be wondering why God gave the
Law if He knew it *would* work against us rather than for us.
God knew that the Law would ultimately work for us when it
brings us to the place He intended for it to. Here are some
astonishing reasons why the Bible reveals God gave the Law.

The first reason is to show man what sin is. Law is a principle which guides our behavior by setting up standards of
conduct and threatening certain consequences if those stan-

dards are not met.

There are several kinds of law set forth in the Bible. There's the "law of conscience" referred to in Romans 2:14,15: **"For when Gentiles who do not have the Law** [of Moses] **do instinctively the things of the Law, these, not having the Law, are a law to themselves, in that they show the work of the Law written in their hearts, their conscience bearing witness, and their thoughts alternately accusing or else defending themselves."**

This law of conscience means that even people who've never heard of the Law of Moses still have an innate law of good and evil and are responsible to live in the light of that.

God rejected the law of conscience as a means for man to see his need for Him because the conscience was too easily seared. By the time Moses came along, the people had so little consciousness of what sin was that God had give to them an objective standard or law that would make clear what sin is.

This was "The Law of Moses." It consisted of not only the Ten Commandments, but also some six hundred laws.

Jesus taught the true meaning of the Ten Commandments in the Sermon on the Mount. Later the Apostles amplified these and added more rules and regulations. These represent still another kind of law — "the law of the New Testament."

All these kinds of law were given for the purpose of defining and showing man what sin is.

The second reason these laws were given was to provoke man's sin nature to sin more. Paul said in Romans 5:20, **"And the Law came in that the transgression might**

increase." God wants the unbeliever to get so loaded with sin that there's no way he can fail to see how utterly sinful he is and how much he needs a Savior.

Paul's personal testimony of his strugle with the Law in Romans chapter seven makes it clear that the Law provokes even the most sincere believer to sin more. He said in verses 7-9 that the Law told him he shouldn't covet (lust), but his sin nature, aroused by that law, produced all the more lust. He said he was once a fruitful, alive believer, with his tendency to lust, well under control. Then all of a sudden he got to dwelling on the fact that the Law said not to lust and lusted all over the place. Trying to keep the commandment actually stirred the sin nature into rebellion. This caused him to die temporarily or to lose fellowship with God. He didn't mean to die physically or to die spiritually. The word "die" here means to cease walking in dependence upon the Holy Spirit, and so *fellowship* with God dies, not relationship.

The third reason God gave the law was to drive us to despair...of self effort. It seems God is working against Himself to get us to sin more, but this is His way of bringing us to total despair of self-effort in seeking to live for Him. You see, the harder we try to keep God's laws, the more we fail. And that's what He intended. The more we fail, the more we have to admit our helplessness and human inadequacy. When we finally get to this kind of despair, we're ready for the fourth reason God gave the Law.

The fourth reason God gave the Law was to bring the unbeliever to Christ for salvation and the believer to the Holy Spirit for His empowering. Paul uses a good illustration of this fact in Galatians 3:24-25, where he says, **"The**

Law has become our tutor to lead us to Christ, that we may be justified by faith. But now that faith has come, we are no longer under a tutor."

A *tutor* was a specially chosen slave whose job it was to take a Roman child by the hand every morning and lead him to the school. He would wait there until the lessons were done and then lead the child home again. Once the child's school days were over, he no longer needed his "tutor."

That's exactly what the Law does, and it was the ultimate purpose of why it was given. The Law takes the unbeliever by the hand and leads him to Christ for salvation. But the Law also takes the believer by the hand and leads him to the Holy Spirit who is the only source of power to do on the inside of us what the Law could never do from without.

THE LAW HAS DONE ITS JOB

So the job of the Law was to show us what sin is and actually make us sin more. Then it was meant to drive us to despair of our self-efforts of trying to keep it, and then to bring us to Christ for salvation, or to bring us to the Holy Spirit so He could produce the righteousness of the Law *in* us. When this progression is finished, then the Law is finally done with the believer.

But, even though the law is through with us, we won't let go of it. In place of the Law of God, we've substituted man-made rules and taboos for how to live the Christian life. Instead of teaching people how to walk in the Spirit, it's been easier to pass rules. This has served only to stimulate the believer's sin nature into greater heights of rebellion. It has *never* produced true righteous living, and it never will. It simply cannot change the heart, nor give us the inner power.

ANARCHY IS NOT FREEDOM

However, it would be folly to go around telling believers that they're no longer responsible to keep God's law unless you also tell them about the grounds of their deliverance from it. Those grounds are twofold.

First, if you'll recall the allegory I started this chapter with, you'll remember that the husband in that story was the Law. When the woman could no longer bear the despair of failure, she allowed herself to be put to death and then raised into a whole new life, legally free and severed from her old husband's authority.

Now, that's just what's happened to each of us in our relationship to the Law. It will never die. But that shouldn't bother us in the least, since we've died to it. Knowing this as a fact is paramount in actually experiencing freedom from the Law. If you don't "reckon" on this deadness, as Paul says in Romans 6, then you'll find yourself being intimidated by law of every kind. Someone will tell a story of how he witnessed to five waitresses and how they all received Christ. Before long you'll feel so guilty about going to a restaurant without witnessing to the waitresses that you'll have trouble eating out.

I often hear people accuse others of putting them under the Law. It's true that some people do wrongly emphasize that as a means of living a Christian life. But if you allow yourself to be put under Law, that's your own fault. God has provided for your freedom from the law principle, and it's up to you to reckon on that deliverance.

THE SPIRIT REPLACED THE LAW

I said there are two reasons why we can tell believers they are no longer responsible to live under the law. The second is, **"If you are led by the Spirit, you are not under the Law"** (Galatians 5:18). The Spirit is our replacement for the Law. He writes the Law in our hearts, that is He puts God's desires in our heart. Then He empowers us to do those desires.

In this same context Paul says, **"Walk by the Spirit, and you will not carry out the desire of the flesh** [sin nature]**"** (Galatians 5:16).

So you can see that freedom from the Law and the sin nature doesn't mean you have no one over you in authority. That is anarchy and it is anything but freedom. Real freedom comes when we submit ourselves to the moment-by-moment control of the indwelling Holy Spirit and allow Him to empower us to live for God.

FREEDOM FROM SATAN'S DOMINATION

The third area in which we've been given our freedom is from Satan's dominion and authority.

One of the great effects of the death of Christ, and your death with Him, is that you were set free from Satan's and demons' authority and control. They can no longer use the old lie, "You must give in to this temptation, because I'm still your master."

The key passage which amplifies this truth is Acts 26:18, in which God says He has opened people's eyes **"...so that they may turn from darkness to light and from the dominion of Satan to God."** The word "dominion" here means "authority." Satan doesn't have any authority or legal right to tell you what to do anymore. Your sin debt was paid by Jesus at the cross, and when He rose from the dead, **"He made you alive together with Him, having forgiven us all our transgressions"** (Colossians 2:13).

The resurrection of Christ proved to be Satan's final undoing. When Jesus rose from the dead, He disarmed the rulers and authorities—referring to Satan and demons — and made a public spectacle of them in showing His triumph over them. He's now the head over all these rulers and authorities. (See Colossians 2:15,10.)

But there's a critical truth here that is not generally understood. Since we were crucified and raised with Christ, His victory over Satan and demons is our victory too. Their legal right to touch us is forever gone.

A clear illustration of this truth is the story that follows. It's a case on record from many years back.

THE CASE OF THE "DEPOSED CAPTAIN"

A ship at sea had a captain so ruthless and brutal to his men that they became desperate and fearful for their safety.

In maritime law, the captain of a ship is the absolute master until officially relieved from command by the country of the ship's registery.

The first mate aboard the vessel was an understanding and humanly sympathetic man, respected by all hands. After much personal consideration and real insistence on the part of the entire crew, he radioed the home port, reporting the atrocities of the captain against his men, and requested permission to assume command at once.

A message was flashed back commissioning him to take official command. The former captain was to be relieved of all authority effective immediately. He was to be held aboard ship and brought home to stand trial. He was allowed freedom to move about on deck, but it was made clear to the entire crew that he had been relieved of his command.

Before long the former captain decided to test his power. A seaman was busy at work, enjoying the leadership of the new captain. The old captain came by, jerked the man up, and began issuing stern orders. The seaman had been so accustomed to following his commands that he instinctively obeyed. And as soon as he started to obey, the old captain proceeded to lay it on all the more.

Amidst the verbal barrage, the seaman came to his senses and realized the man no longer had authority over him. He began to resist — and got the beating of his life. Bruised and battered, he told his rightful commander of the incident.

The new captain told him that if the former commander tried this again, to call him and he would take care of the old captain.

SET FREE TO SERVE

Let's face it. We're at war. But God wants us to know that we no longer have to give in to the demands of our sin natures. We are no longer under the law, and we have been liberated from the authority and dominion of Satan. The ransom was paid by Jesus, and we've been set free from the slave market of sin. The only slavery for us now is our willing slavery to Jesus out of love and gratitude.

A wonderful story illustrates this.

In the days of slavery in ancient Rome, a notorious and cruel slave holder was in the Roman slave market to purchase some additional slaves. That particular day there was a stranger there also. He was a kindly man who was new to the market. He bought slaves in order to set them free.

A slave was put up on the dock, and the bidding started. The cruel man opened the bid, and the good man immediately set forth a counter bid. The prices offered began to soar to dizzy heights as the men bid back and forth.

Finally the good man named a price so high that the wicked slave holder couldn't match it.

As the new owner walked up to the auctioneer of the slave market to pay the ransom, the slave marched over behind his new master and prepared to follow him.

The good man who had bought the slave turned around and said, "You're free to go. I bought you to set you free." And he started to walk away.

"Wait a minute," the slave answered. "If I'm a free man, then I'm free to follow you. My desire is to serve you out of gratitude for what you've done for me."

What this slave experienced is just what Christ has done for us. He has set us free from the impossible demands of the Law. He's purchased us out of Satan's slave market and stripped him of his authority over us. And He has delivered us from the tyranny of our sin natures by giving us a new nature and the indwelling Holy Spirit to fight it.

But not only has Jesus Christ set our *spirits* free through His redemption, He's also provided for the ultimate redemption of our *bodies* (Romans 8:23). He has already paid the ransom price for the redemption of our physical bodies. The resurrection of our physical bodies will come when the Lord Jesus returns — and I believe that is very near indeed.

God doesn't demand that we become His servants, but Paul says it's the only reasonable thing to do in light of all God has done for us.

---

1. *Satan Is Alive and Well on Planet Earth* (Grand Rapids: Zondervan Publishing House, 1972).

CHAPTER 17

REGENERATION:

A NEW BIRTH

You have made us for Yourself, O God,
And our hearts are restless
Until they find their rest in You.

—AUGUSTINE

Every spring the whole earth gives illustration of regeneration as the plants emerge from their wintry slumber and sprout forth fresh, green vegetation. Plant life is reborn or given new life. What has been dead for a time now comes back to life.

It is fascinating to put a kernel of corn into the ground and to see new life spring forth from it. Yet there is a far greater miracle — the regeneration of the human spirit that has been made possible through Christ's substitutionary death on the cross. The moment we place our trust in Christ's death on our behalf, the Holy Spirit of God impregnates our dead human spirits with the eternal life of God and we're reborn spiritually.

One of the clearest declarations of man's need to be born again (literally "born from above") is a conversation Jesus had with Israel's leading religious teacher, Nicodemus. This was a sincere and humanly righteous man. The fact that he sought Jesus out shows he was seeking after God and His kingdom.

In this conversation Jesus revealed one of the most important truths He ever taught. Man must have a new spiritual birth before he can understand the truth about God and His kingdom.

"Now there was a man of the Pharisees, named Nicodemus, a ruler of the Jews; this man came to Him [Jesus] by night, and said to Him, 'Rabbi, we know that You have come from God as

a teacher; for no one can do these signs that You
do unless God is with him.'

"Jesus answered and said to him, 'Truly, truly,
I say to you, unless one is born again *[from above]*,
he cannot see the kingdom of God.'

"Nicodemus said to Him, 'How can a man be
born when he is old? He cannot enter a second
time into his mother's womb and be born, can
he?'

"Jesus answered, 'Truly, truly, I say to you,
unless one is born of water and the Spirit, he cannot enter into the kingdom of God. That which is
born of the flesh is flesh; and that which is born of
the Spirit is spirit.

"'Do not marvel that I said to you, "You must
be born again."

"'The wind blows where it wishes and you
hear the sound of it, but do not know where it
comes from and where it is going; so is every one
who is born of the Spirit'" (John 3:1-8).

THE RE-EDUCATION OF NICODEMUS

Nicodemus's response to what Jesus said was simple
and straightforward: "How can these things be?"

"Jesus answered and said to him, 'Are you *the*
teacher of Israel, and do not understand these things?'"
(John 3:9,10). "You mean to say, Nicodemus, that you're the
leading teacher of Israel and you have never realized that
there was a spiritual dimension missing from man?"

You see, Nicodemus prided himself that he was born
into the race of God's chosen people. He was banking his
eventual salvation too heavily on his physical heritage.

That's why Jesus went right to the real issue and pulled the rug out from under him. In essence, what He told Nicodemus was that His vast education had not equipped him to even know the elementary things about God and His Kingdom.

MANKIND "ISN'T ALL THERE!"

I'm sure you've already noticed that something's desperately wrong with people in this world. A casual glance at the morning news is enough to put you under a gloom cloud all day. Nothing but murders, scandal, war, crooked politicians, divorces, and so forth.

The thing that is wrong with people is they aren't all there. The most important dimension of their being is missing, their human spirit. Without it, nothing functions the way God designed us to live.

In chapter six on Spiritual Death, there is a diagram of the three parts of man — spirit, soul, and body. In this chapter I will show how they work in a believer. It is impera-

BORN AGAIN BELIEVER

tive to have a clear understanding of how these three parts of our being function, or we will not be able to find the source of problems when things go wrong.

THE CREATION OF MAN'S TWO KINDS OF LIFE

When God made our physical body, He fashioned it from the elements of the ground. Then He breathed into the first man's physical body the breath of lives, and man became a living soul (Genesis 2:7).

Two kinds of life were born that day, *soulish life* (*psuche* — ψυχη) which started the heart beating and blood flowing and the mind and personality of man. And *spiritual life* (*zoe* — ζωη) which became the human spirit in man that enabled him to know and communicate with God who is spirit. These two kinds of life were placed in the physical body of man, and there was harmony in their interworkings.

The Bible says man became a "living soul" (KJV). The soul was to stand in the center, between the spirit and body, and be the merging place of these two. It was to be the part of man through which the spirit and body expressed themselves. It stood between these two worlds, yet it belonged integrally to both. Since the soul has free will, it was to decide which would dominate the life, the spirit or the body.

Before Adam sinned, the spirit dominated his soul and body. But with his free will, which was part of his personality in the soul, Adam made the decision to disobey God. The instant death of Adam and Eve's soul caused a catastrophic inner change. Their capacity to communicate with God ceased, and a deadness developed in man's relationship with God. The soul still had the memory of fellowship with God, but it was not adequate to have the intimacy they had known. The tragic result of this was that the soul and body of man was now left without a means of spiritual perception. Their whole consciousness *excluded* the enlightening and restraining power of God.

Instead of being "God" centered, man became "self" centered. Instead of being a "flower" out of the Creator's hand, he became a "weed" growing wild, with no cultivation or grooming.

Let's look at each one of these functions of man separately now, using the diagram on the next page to help visualize these critical truths.

THE SPIRIT

From the moment man sinned, his only hope was regeneration. When Adam and Eve were created, they were given a human spirit that enabled them to commune with God. However, their human spirit did *not* contain the everlasting type life of God.

In the middle of the Garden, where it couldn't be overlooked, was the Tree of Life. This was available for man to eat anytime he wanted to. I believe if our first parents had chosen to, they would have received eternal life.

But there was another tree there also, the Tree of Knowledge of Good and Evil. We've already seen in past chapters that this tree was the "test" tree. Man was forbidden to eat of it. To do so meant he was vaunting his will over God's and rejecting the relationship (Genesis 2:17).

IT TOOK DEATH TO DESTROY DEATH . . .

After man ate from the tree, God said, "**"Behold, the man has become like one of Us, knowing good and evil;**

and now, lest he stretch out his hand, and take also from the tree of life, and eat, and live forever...' he must be sent out of the Garden and his way back to the Tree of Life prohibited" (Genesis 3:22-24).

God couldn't let man be perpetuated in a state of spiritual death. Death was a necessary intregal part of God's plan to redeem man from his terrible condition. As strange as it may seem, it took a death to destroy death — the death of the precious Son of God.

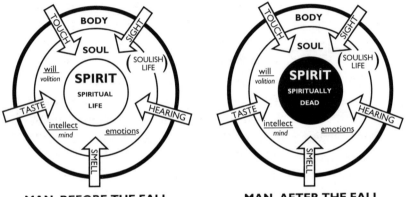

MAN, BEFORE THE FALL   **MAN, AFTER THE FALL**

THE RENOVATION OF THE SPIRIT

The rebirth of your spirit begins the day you believe in the substitutionary death of Jesus for you. Some people like to use the concept of inviting Jesus to come into their heart. That's based on Jesus' statement in Revelation 3:20, **"Behold, I stand at the door and knock; if any one hears My voice and opens the door, I will come in to him, and will dine [fellowship] with him, and he with Me."** This *door* represents your will.

But whatever you understood at the moment you received Christ as Savior, the most important thing is that your dead human spirit was "born from above" and the Holy Spirit came to dwell in it.

The great French philosopher and theologian, Pascal, called this spiritual void in man before the new birth a "God-shaped vacuum which only Christ could fill."

THE DEAD SPIRIT DOES SERVE A FUNCTION

This vacuum in the unbeliever plays an important role. It serves as a constant reminder that something very basic is missing from our inner beings. Augustine described it this way, "You have made us for yourself, O God, and our hearts are restless until they find their rest in You."

Until the One who made us comes to dwell in His rightful place in our spirits, we will never feel complete. There will always be a sense of something missing. This accounts for why so many people give themselves to hedonism. In an effort to find inner fulfillment and peace, they frantically pursue sex, money, fame, power, position, beauty, pleasure, religion, and even the occult. Even the "do gooders" without Christ are simply trying to fill their sense of an inner vacuum.

THE LIGHT IN MEN COMES BACK ON

The Bible pictures the unregenerate man as "walking in darkness." That is why he cannot understand that all the things he tries to substitute for Jesus in his life are only delusive counterfeits. When Adam sinned, spiritual darkness filled the vacuum left by his dead spirit. His spiritual light was gone.

But at the heart of God's plan to regenerate men was His intention of restoring His light to this darkened void. Jesus lamented this catastrophic spiritual darkness in men, **"If therefore the light that is in you is darkness, how great is the darkness"** (Matthew 6:23b).

The Apostle John revealed that Jesus would bring the light back to men. **"In Him** [Jesus] **was life; and the life was the *light* of men...**[He] **was the true light which, coming into the world, enlightens** [sheds light on] **every man"** (John 1:4,9).

Peter said that Jesus was the One who has **"...called you out of darkness into His marvelous light"** (1 Peter 2:9b).

But the greatest authority on the subject of "light" was Jesus Himself. He called Himself **"the light of the world; He who follows Me shall not walk in the darkness,"** He said, **"but shall have the light of life"** (John 8:12).

So when a person is born again, the light really goes on inside him. For the first time he's able to understand the things of God and perceive the spiritual realm. And God begins to shine that new light onto his path and show him His will.

WALK AS "CHILDREN OF LIGHT"

It's because we've been given this inner light that Paul admonishes us the way he does in Ephesians 5:1-8. There he talks about a number of sins that unregenerate men freely participate in: greed, immorality, silly and dirty talk, coveting, and so forth. Then he says, **"Do not be partakers with them, for you were formerly darkness, but now you are light in the Lord; walk as children of light"** (verses 7, 8).

I think that's a terrific description of born-again believers — "Children of Light." If there's anything this dark old world needs, it's light. You can see that by the fantastic rise in popularity of psychics, astrologers, prophets, and others trying to find out what's going on. But the only true source of light as to where the world's going, and how to be prepared to live at peace in the world, is the "Children of Light." That's why Jesus said, **"Let your light shine before men in such a way that they may see your good works, and glorify your Father who is in heaven"** (Matthew 5:16).

Let's take a look now at the main function of the regenerated spirit.

THE SIXTH SENSE: FAITH

When a man is born again, he is given new spiritual life and a new spiritual nature is created within him. For the first time he is able to understand divine phenomena and to know God personally. And the things of the spiritual realm are no longer unreal and alien. The Holy Spirit takes up residence in his spiritual nature and begins to reveal the truth of God to him.

This restoration of spiritual life gives back to man what Adam lost. It's like a "sixth sense." Faith is the eyesight of this new spiritual nature. It enables us to reach out to God and to know Him as a person. Faith enables us to believe that when God says He will do something for us, He absolutely will.

The body has its five senses through which the soul relates to the material world and establishes its sense of reality. The total of knowledge gained through these senses is called the "human viewpoint" of life (HVP for short). But the intimate knowledge of God can only be known through the new nature working through the sixth sense, faith. This is called the "divine viewpoint" of life (DVP for short).

Only the person who's been born again has a sixth sense and thus he has both these viewpoints in him (DVP). The unregenerate person has only the human viewpoint (HVP).

These two viewpoints of life are very often in conflict with each other. The five senses continually pour into the mind the world's view on everything. This viewpoint says man determines his own destiny and God is not a relevant force.

On the other hand, the sixth sense says, "Look, God made you. He put you together atom by atom. Even though you excluded Him from your life, He loves you and provided redemption for you. Now don't you think you can trust a God like that to handle whatever your problems are?"

And so, both the recreated human spirit *(the sixth sense)* and the flesh *(the five senses)* bombard the soul *(mind)* with their viewpoints, and these two are almost always opposed to one another.

For example, Paul promises the believers that **"God causes all things to work together for good to those who love God"** (Romans 8:28). Now, suppose when you walked into work this morning, your boss met you and said you were fired. Through the senses of sight and hearing, this is *(humanly speaking)* very bad news. At the same time, through your sixth sense of faith, God reminded you of His promise that He will work even this together for good.

At this point you must decide which viewpoint of life you are going to let dominate you. If the HVP dominates, you'll probably panic and go into depression. But if you choose to believe what your the sixth sense reveals, you will experience the peace of God that surpasses all under-standing (of the HVP). You will operate on the DVP, which says that God has promised to provide your needs and to guide you. Remember the DVP commandment, "Thou shalt not sweat it."

FAITH DEPENDS ON GOD'S FAITHFULNESS

The best way to understand faith is this: It is our response to God's ability to cope with our problems through us. If I really believe He's able, then I'll automatically have faith. If I don't know how trustworthy He is, then no amount of spiritual gimmickry is going to make me trust Him when I need to.

Faith is such a misunderstood concept. I often hear people praying for more faith, but strictly speaking, that's a wrong prayer. Once you've been born again and had your sixth sense restored to your spirit, you have all the faith potential you need.

THE RELATION OF *FAITH* AND ITS *OBJECT*

The power is not in our faith, but in the *object* of our faith. The more I come to understand how loving and power-ful God is, the more I will place my little faith in Him. Jesus said, **"I tell you the truth, if you have *faith as small as* a mustard seed, you can say to this mountain, 'Move from here to there' and it will move. Nothing will be impossible for you"** (Matthew 17:20 NIV).

To look at it from another angle, faith operates in your re-born spirit just as the five senses operate in your body. Take the sense of sight, for example. You can have

20/20 vision and yet look at a mountain fifty miles away and not see it very clearly. What's the problem? You don't need better eyesight — you need to get closer to the mountain so you can see it better.

That's the way faith works. We are all given 20/20 faith when we're born again. But faith needs an object in order for it to function, and God, revealed to us through His Word, is the object.

If Jesus has not seemed as real to you as you might want, and you've felt that you needed more faith to bring Him closer, then what you really need is to get a closer view of this wonderful Object. You do this by getting into His Word, especially focusing on what He did for you on the cross. Then His promises will become believable. Technically your faith does not grow, but your concept of Jesus does. The end result will be a new certainty of the unseen sphere God dwells and operates in. You will believe Him more. You will also find yourself loving and responding to Him in a way you never thought possible.

THE SOUL

Whereas the spirit is that part of man which makes him conscious of God and relates him to Him, the soul is that part of us which relates us to ourselves and gives us self-consciousness. Then through the function of God's image in the soul — will, intellect, emotion and conscience or moral reason — we are able to form a world view and give expression to our inner selves.

The soul enables us to reveal our personalities. It draws upon both the conscious and subconscious minds which are part of it. It is the part of man through which the spirit and body find their external expression.

In the Bible people are occasionally referred to as "souls." This is because God views the soul as the man himself. A man without a soul is a dead man because the soul is the actual life in us. The Hebrew word for soul, *nephesh,* is often translated "life" in the Old Testament. The New Testament uses the Greek word *psuche* for both "soul" and "soul life" and it is also often translated as "life."

"The *life* [soul] of the flesh is in the blood" (Leviticus 17:11).

"I do not consider my *life* [soul] of any account..." (Acts 20:24).

"The good shepherd lays down His *life* [soul] for the sheep" (John 10:11).

ADAM "BLEW IT," BUT HE WAS NO DUMMY!

When we are born into this world, the only kind of life we have is soulish life (*psuche*). That's what we educate, train, discipline, pamper, and eagerly protect. The power in a human soul is not unlimited, but it's certainly very great.

When you stop to think about the fantastic degree of intelligence Adam had in his soul, it makes you believe a little bit more in the *downward* spiral of mankind's mind, not the upward climb.

Adam was given dominion over the whole earth and everything in it (Genesis 1:27, 28). It took tremendous organizational skill and know-how to accomplish just that task. But that was not his only privilege. He also named all the animals and species of life. We have whole societies today that try to keep up with just parts of the many species on this planet. Yet Adam named and knew about all of them.

Adam was also a skilled gardener. He was entrusted
with the upkeep of the Garden of Eden. I know what a job it
is just to try to keep my own small garden fertilized, pruned,
and groomed. But the size of the Garden of Eden must have
been staggering. Yet, it did not seem to be a problem for
Adam. He never knew what it was to sweat until he was dri-
ven from the Garden and his soul's great powers began to
deteriorate. (See Genesis 3:19.)

MAN'S SELF-CENTEREDNESS BEGINS

From Adam's capabilities, we can see what God must
have originally had in mind for our soulish life.
Unfortunately, when Adam sinned, the soul was no longer
under the control of the spirit, and so all it could do was
become more and more *self*-conscious and *self*-centered.
Men began to think only about themselves — of how to meet
their own needs and fulfill their own carnal appetites. The
soul — which had been intended by God to be the place of
the balanced expression of the complete man, *body, soul,* and
spirit — now became the center of the fallen "ego" or "self."

DYNAMICS OF A "SOULISH MAN"

The Apostle Paul coined a name for man in this condition. He called him, "the soulish man" (1 Corinthians
2:14). That's because the soul, with its will, mind and emotions, capitulated completely to the desires of the sin nature.
In this same verse Paul reveals the limitations of the soulish
man; **"But a natural man** [literally, a "soulish man"] **does
not accept the things of the Spirit of God; for they are
foolishness to him, and he cannot understand them,**

because they are spiritually appraised." The word *psuchikos* (ψυχικο), translated "natural," is the adjective form of the Greek word *psuche* (ψυχη). It means literally "the man characterized by only a soul." This is why a man who is not born again can not understand or accept the simplest things of the spiritual realm. He may have multiple Ph.D.s, but still have no spiritual discernment. It is not a matter of intelligence, but of not having the right kind of life.

THE BODY

So far we have briefly studied the makeup of the spirit and soul in man. Now let us look at the body, or flesh, of mankind and see its role in the whole man.

The body is the material part of our being through which the soul and spirit express themselves. It is the house of the soul and spirit. It is intimately united with the soul because it (the *psuche*) keeps the physical body alive. After the fall of man, the soul and body became increasingly bonded to the material world. If a person's soul was dominant, he would tend to be more artistic, philosophical and intellectual. If the body dominated, then the person tended to be more sensuous or athletic.

The five senses located in the physical body are the mechanisms which bring the reality of the material world into the consciousness of the person. They're like windows of the soul. In order for the senses to operate, however, they must have an external stimulus of some kind. For example, there has to be an object in order for sight to function. Likewise, there has to be a sound in order for hearing to occur, and so forth.

One of the basic principles that many psychologists

teach is that man is a product of his environment. This means we are simply the sum total of all the things that have touched our lives. All the experiences and forces that have molded our lives have come into us through the agency of the five senses. Of course, the way we handle the phenomena that comes into our minds is influenced greatly by our inherited temperaments and traits. And once we become believers, the indwelling Holy Spirit influences our reactions to the things that happen to us.

THE FLESH IS NO FRIEND OF GOD

As I have said before, the actual substance of the flesh is not usually what that word means in the Bible. It often refers to a principle of rebellion against God that's permeated all of fallen mankind. It is so unreformable that God did not even try to salvage it. The sinful nature or flesh is somehow a part of our physical bodies. This is why God cannot remove it until we either die physically or are translated directly into the new immortal body by the Rapture. (See 1 Corinthians 15:50-54.)

So God pronounced the "flesh" hopelessly rebellious and then proceeded to put a new spiritual nature in us through the miracle of regeneration.

Whatever is wrapped up in the concept of the flesh, all men have it. The frightening truth is that it is the *only* realm in which unregenerate men can operate.

Listen to how the Apostle Paul viewed the matter of the flesh as he wrote to the believers at Ephesus. **"And you were dead in your trespasses and sins, in which you formerly walked according to the course of this world, according to the prince of the power of the air** [atmosphere of thought], **of the spirit that is now working in the sons of disobedience. Among them we too all formerly lived in the** *lusts of our flesh* **indulging the** *desires of the flesh* **and of the mind, and were by nature children of wrath, even as the rest"** (Ephesians 2:1-3).

As much as some people might not like to think about it, God has a very dim view of the flesh — whether it's in a believer or an unbeliever.

The Bible tells us that the flesh is hostile to God — that anyone who is dominated by the flesh cannot please God (Romans 8:7,8).

God also tells us that even a believer whose mind is habitually controlled by the flesh is temporarily operating in the sphere of spiritual death (Romans 8:6).

Even the great Apostle Paul shared the problem he still had with the flesh, **"For I know that nothing good dwells in me,** *that is, in my flesh"* (Romans 7:18).

These verses and many more reveal there is a "fallenness" in us that comes from the flesh. This rebellious nature is sometimes spoken of as "sin," as in 1 John 1:8: **"If we say that we have no sin, we are deceiving ourselves, and the truth is not in us."**

The flesh is also synonymous with the Old Sin Nature which as we've already seen, is that force in us which is dedicated to resisting God.

THE TWO SIDES OF THE FLESH

At the Fall, the body and soul merged together to comprise this spiritual foe we know as the flesh. It includes the "attitudes of the flesh" as well as the "works of the flesh." These two sides of the flesh will continue to manifest themselves in the believer to the degree that he allows his soul to dominate him, rather than his spirit.

ATTITUDES OF THE FLESH

The "attitudes of the flesh" are all the ideas, plans, schemes, imaginations, and good works which proceed out of the human mind without the Holy Spirit being the source of them. They can be either good or bad, as the world views such things, but in God's estimation they're all unacceptable because the flesh is the source of them, not the spirit. These "attitudes of the flesh" are sometimes hard to detect because they deal in the realm of ideas and thoughts and often seem so noble. However, these soulish activities always have self somewhere at the center.

Self-confidence and *self*-reliance are two notable traits of the soul. The world applauds these and they seem like such admirable qualities, but God says they indicate a reliance on the flesh rather than on the indwelling Holy Spirit.

The "works of the flesh" are often referred to as the "lusts of the flesh," and these refer to the sins which are stimulated by the fleshy drives and passions. These are fairly easy to spot in a life because they're usually pretty gross and overt. Paul lists some of them, **"Now the *deeds of the flesh* are evident, which are: immorality, impurity, sensuality, idolatry, sorcery, enmities, strife, jealousy, outbursts of anger, disputes, dissension, factions, envying, drunkenness, carousings, and things like these"** (Galatians 5:19-21).

THE FLESH IS TRICKY

Believers get tripped up by not realizing that the flesh is not only the *sin*-tendency, but also the *self*-tendency. It's easier to spot the overt sins that originate out of the desires and demands of the flesh. But the "attitude" sins of the flesh are much more subtle and more "socially acceptable" in the Christian community. But the Lord knows the source of the attitude sins, and He holds the one committing them responsible.

For instance, as a young believer I heard many sermons by preachers and Sunday school teachers about the sinfulness of drinking, smoking, dancing, and going to movies. But I never heard a sermon about the evils of teaching a Sunday school class while not filled with the Spirit.

These are the more subtle works of the flesh of which only God and you know whether He's the source. But if God is not the source, then those "good deeds" are just as repugnant to Him as all the overt sins on the official Southern Baptist "taboo list."

THE RENOVATION OF REGENERATION

One of my favorite songs has the first line, "I believe in miracles, I've seen a soul set free."

To me, with all the emphasis on miracles in the Church today, the greatest one is God's salvation work of undoing the internal damage to man's spirit, soul, and body and bringing back the original harmony and balance.

Paul amplifies this when he says, **"Therefore if any man is in Christ, he is a new creature; the old things passed away; behold, new things have come"** (2 Corinthians 5:17).

What were those old things that passed away?

Basically, your "Old Man" passed away. *(May he rest in peace!)* That's everything you were in Adam — spiritually dead, hostile to God, under the Law, headed for eternity in hell, a slave of Satan, dominated by your soulish life and the flesh, unrighteous and self-centered, etc.

The Apostle Paul taught that the crucifixion of the "Old Man" was the basis of breaking the power of all those things we were in Adam: **"Knowing this, that our old man was crucified with Christ, that our body with its sin nature might be made powerless, that we should no longer be slaves to sin; for he who has died is justified regarding the sin nature"** (Romans 6:6,7 translated from original Greek HL).

But as I said in the last chapter, there is no power in simply being dead. We went into the grave as the "Old Man," but through union with Christ our "New Man" was raised into His resurrection life. Paul stresses this in his letter to the Colossians. He tells the believers to keep setting their minds on things above, not on the things of earth, for they *have* died to those things and are simply to consider it as a fact. He urges believers to put aside things like anger, wrath, ill-will, dirty language, and lies, because they have laid aside the Old Man *(self)* with its evil practices and *have* put on the New Man *(self)* who is in the process of being renewed into the image of God by the indwelling Spirit. (See Colossians 3:1-3.)

HOW TO BECOME WHAT YOU *ARE* IN CHRIST

God declares the old things passed away when we were born again, and that all things became new. This is already true by a divine fiat. What God declares in His Word to be true of me is the most true thing there is, whether I feel it or not.

Because of our union with Christ, all things *are* new in our eternal standing before God. These new things *become* true in our experience when we claim them as true by faith. Then the Holy Spirit makes them manifest in our experience.

In actual behavior, all things have not yet become new. We still have many of the same old hang-ups and soul-kinks we had before we were born again. But as we discover and believe who we are in Christ, we progressively see the "new man" manifested.

HE WON OUR VICTORY— NOW WE MUST CLAIM IT

Regeneration created our new spiritual life the moment we believed in Christ. But the repercussions progressively take place throughout our whole being. Our souls and bodies come under the rightful domination of the spirit as we grow into maturity. This is one of the great purposes of regeneration — to bring our body, soul, and spirit back into the original unity and harmony God designed.

From the moment we are born again, our spirits are indwelt by the Holy Spirit of God. He is the actual agent of change for our new life.

This is such an important part of salvation that God warns if you do not have the Spirit in you, you do not belong to Christ (Romans 8:9).

But whether the Holy Spirit is allowed to fill (control) our soul and flesh is a matter of personal daily choice. The soul still has free will, and it must decide moment by moment what will dominate the life — the Holy Spirit, living through our reborn spirit, or the flesh (sin).

It is to our free will that Paul makes his plea, **"*Consider yourselves* to be dead to sin...Do *not let* sin reign in your mortal body...*Do not go on presenting* the members of your body to sin as instruments of unright-eousness"** (Romans 6:11-13).

These are commands that can be ignored or followed.

Our responsibility is to *choose* to believe and obey, and then the Spirit goes into action and pours the power into us to *do* what we have believed. We are never relieved of the responsibility of *choosing* to follow the Father's will, but the actual power to *do it* comes from the Holy Spirit. That is what Paul meant when he said, **"For it is God who works in you, both to will and to do"** (Philippians 2:13 NKJV). The *willing* part comes from the presence of the New Nature within us, and the *doing* comes from the power of the indwelling Holy Spirit. The choice of faith is ours.

OBEDIENCE AND THE SPIRIT'S POWER

A lot of believers want the *power* to come before they move out in response to the commands of the Word. They want to see, feel, and experience the victory before they take the steps of faith into the battle. That really amounts to walking by sight and not by faith. True faith only needs the *promise* that God will fight for us. The flesh demands visible proof before it can believe.

Joshua and Israel were commanded to attack the Canaanites before God would fight for them. He went before them and gave them victory as they took each step of faith.

This truth is often confusing to believers who are just beginning to learn to walk by faith. They don't want to run ahead of the Lord. So, when they read certain commands in the Word, they wait for some strong motivation and almost physical "shove" from the Holy Spirit before they move into action.

Many keep singing "Standing on the promises" while sitting on the premises.

You can't steer a car unless it is moving, and the Holy

Spirit can't force you into action unless you have made the decision to step out into whatever God has revealed to you is His will. For instance, we know it's God's will that we love one another because His Word teaches that (John 13:34). He doesn't tell us to have the "emotion" of love for one another. He tells us to "love" one another, and that is a verb. It is something you choose to do, not something that you necessarily *feel*.

So what do we do when by nature we dislike someone? Do we ask the Spirit to give us the emotion of love for him or her — then keep on hating until we are hit by some divine spurt of love?

No! I believe we already know it's God's will to *demonstrate* love to our brothers and sisters — not necessarily *feel* it. And we know that if God wills something, then He give us His enabling power as we believe Him and obey.

So trusting Him to empower us to *show* love, whether we "feel" it or not, we begin to demonstrate love to the person. We don't bad-mouth him to others. We begin to be sensitive to his needs and try to look at things from his point of view. We take time to show him kindnesses, and we simply accept him in the same way that God has accepted us.

Now, as we do these things, our attitude of faith is that He must take care of the consequences of our actions and turn our "demonstration" of love into a true "feelings" of love.

There's a three-step progression: TRUST, OBEY, EXPECT.

First, we simply *trust* that what God has called us to do, or to cease doing, is His best and highest plan for us, because we know He loves us.

Second, in the light of that knowledge, and with the

promise that what He's called us to do He'll give us the power to, we *obey* His will.

Third, we *expect* Him to keep His end of the bargain and empower us to do that which we have moved into by faith.

THE TWO KINDS OF BELIEVERS

Now, you would think that once a man was born again, he'd be so thankful to have his relationship with God restored that he would gladly and consistently live in dependence upon the Holy Spirit.

But this is not the case with many believers. The soul *(self)* has held sway over us for so many years, that there's a lot of unlearning and learning to do. Our minds must be renewed, as Paul tells us in Romans 12:2, in order that we might be transformed in our behavior. We have already been given a nature created in the image of God. (See Ephesians 4:24.) So now we need to bring our behavior in line with what God has made us. This is where the need for the power of the Holy Spirit comes in. *We* cannot transform ourselves, but the Holy Spirit can as He applies the cleansing and renewing power of the Word of God to our lives.

This, of course, necessitates that we spend time reading and studying the Bible. For as the Psalmist prayed, **"Thy Word I have treasured in my heart, that I may not sin against Thee"** (Psalm 119:11).

The believer who consistently allows himself to be renewed in his mind and spirit by the Holy Spirit, is a "spiritual man" (1 Corinthians 3:1). This doesn't mean that he is a perfect, sinless man. But it does mean that he is characterized by being preoccupied with the things of God and the spirit.

When he sins, he confesses it to God and quickly claims forgiveness. Then he turns again to walk by faith.

There is another kind of believer discussed in 1
Corinthians 3. This one is still a babe in Christ, even though
he may have been a true believer for years. He is all caught
up with the things of the world, and he's still living like the
old soulish man he used to be. The flesh is the dominant factor in his life. Paul calls this believer "carnal" or "fleshly."

The New Testament Epistles give a composite picture
of a carnal believer. It would do us all good to check this list
and see if any of this applies to us. All believers will have
some of these things in their lives occasionally, yet they
couldn't honestly be categorized as "carnal." But if *many* of
these things are true of you, I sincerely urge you to consider
the possibility that you may be a carnal believer. You may
need to confess and turn from some sin in your life. Then to
claim the power of the Holy Spirit to cleanse and renew you.

Carnal Believers...

. . . argue and reason about most things

. . . are self-righteous and defensive about their actions

. . . can't concentrate on spiritual things for long

. . . are up and down emotionally

. . . are overly sensitive

. . . are talkative, always having to be at the center of each
       conversation and usually dominate it

. . . give in to lust of the eyes; are always buying things

. . . have an unbalanced emphasis on sex

. . . have a poor prayer life

. . . are undisciplined

. . . are easily discouraged

. . . when it comes to preaching, can't rely wholly on God, but
       fill up their sermons with illustrations, stories, and jokes

. . . are proud, because self is their center

. . . thrive on the sensational, because they're not sure people
     will be duly impressed with them if they don't

. . . are critical of fellow believers

. . . have a poor family life

. . . are braggers

. . . engage in frivolous and suggestive jesting

. . . are intemperate in eating and drinking

. . . indulge in swearing and dirty talk

. . . have no desire for the Word

. . . give in to jealousy and strife.

Paul sums up the carnal believer's problem by saying,
"You're walking like mere men" (1 Corinthians 3:3b).

And there is the tragedy, because believers are not
supposed to be like "mere men." "Mere men" aren't all there.
They have only a body and a soul — their spirit is dead.
They are not *normal* human beings, but they don't realize it
because everyone else is just like them.

The exception is the spiritual believer who walks by
faith, allowing the spirit to have the rightful role of dominance in his life. This one is "normal" because that's how
God made man to function.

SUMMING IT ALL UP

When the subject of regeneration is taught, it's usually related just to the work of God in giving new life to our
dead human spirits and imparting the Holy Spirit to dwell in
us. I hope you have seen from this chapter that there's much
more involved in God's miracle of regeneration. It's actually
the work of God giving balance and harmony to the whole
man once again. The spirit of man is put back into its rightful

place of dominance in us. And the soul and flesh that got us so out of hand with no inner restraint, are gradually brought back under the authority of the Holy Spirit.

So regeneration means God has made us whole people again. He has equipped us to live victoriously in this life and gloriously with Him in eternity.

"Not by works of righteousness which we have done, but according to His mercy He saved us, through the washing of regeneration and renewing of the Holy Spirit" (Titus 3:5 NKJV).

CHAPTER 18

NEW POSITION

CREATURES OF ETERNITY

LIVING IN TIME

T his final truth reveals the ultimate of what God's grace through the cross does for the believer. Virtually everything God does for the believer is through our total union with His Son, which is our NEW POSITION before God in eternity.

I'm convinced this truth is understood by few believers and that's why the majority of the church today doesn't have the vitality and power of the First Century church.

In the last hundred years a number of books have appeared which have dealt with this concept in one way or another. The believer's new position in Christ has made possible an intimate relationship with Him which has been called by many names: the Deeper Life, the Abiding Life, the Higher Life, the Crucified Life, the Exchanged Life, the Spirit-filled Life, the Victorious Life, the Baptism of the Spirit, Identification With Christ, and Union With Christ.

Such writers as Jesse Penn Lewis, Ruth Paxson, Fritz Huegel, Charles Trumbull, E. W. Kenyon, Watchman Nee, Major Ian Thomas, L. S. Chafer, Miles Stanford, Andrew Murray and Robert Thieme, Jr. are among the many whose books have given greater clarity and insight into the liberating results of the believer's new position in Christ. I first learned about these marvelous truths through Robert Thieme, who was my pastor at the time. I still remember the spiritual exhilaration from the realization that I was already a creature of eternity, seated at the right hand of God's throne in Christ.

No matter what name we choose to call this truth, there can be little doubt that there is a life of great spiritual depth, power, and victory available to all believers that is actually experienced by only a few.

I got a deeper understanding of this truth while teaching for Campus Crusade for Christ in Mexico City. A master of this doctrine, a theologian named Dr. Fritz Huegel, spent many hours walking about Mexico City with me in December of 1967 and January of 1968. I was so privileged to receive the distilled essence of his personal experience of this truth, which he proved in his experience through more than forty years on the mission fields of Latin America.

In this chapter we will see why our union with Christ is the basis for consistent and victorious Christian living.

THE SEARCH FOR THE "DEEPER" LIFE

You don't have to be a believer for long before you discover by personal experience that *being* a Christian and *living* like one are often different things. As the Apostle Paul wrote of his experience in Romans chapter seven, we find that we want to do the right thing while continuing to do the very thing we hate.

When we experience the conflict of our dual natures, many of us simply feel the struggle is too great. Many give in to the up-and-down Christian life and settle into spiritual mediocrity. Others endure the struggle and seek to find God's provision for living above the pull of the world, the flesh, and the devil.

Many of these sincere souls, while looking for this

· "deeper" life, have been led on strange pilgrimages by well-meaning Chrisitians.   Unfortunately, a number come away with no lasting answers and more frustration. That's because what they're looking for isn't located in some higher or deeper place, or in some ecstatic experience. It's located in a person, Jesus Christ.

The *deeper, higher, victorious, abiding, exchanged, and Spirit-filled life* is not an elusive, wishful aspiration. It's simply a matter of living with the moment-by-moment awareness that because of my absolute oneness with Jesus in the eyes of God, all that He is, *I am.* His victory over sin *is my victory over sin.* He's holy and blameless in the eyes of the Father and *so am I.* Satan no longer has any authority over Him, and *he has no authority over me either.* He's more than conqueror, and God's Word testifies to me that *I am too.* Christ was crucified, buried, raised from the dead, and is now seated at God's right hand. In the mind of God, *each true believer went through these same experiences* with Christ and *is now seated in the heavenlies* in Christ, regardless of where his actual physical body may be located here on earth at the moment.

In other words, my new position in Christ gives me a *total* identification with Jesus in God's eyes. As He looks at the Son, He looks at me in the same way because He sees me *in* the Son and the Son *in* me.

If I take a grimy piece of paper, insert it into the pages of a book and close it, that paper is identified with the book and we can no longer see it. We only see the book. Because Christ removed the barriers separating God and man, the one who has received Him as Savior is inseparably united or fused into Christ and Christ into Him. What becomes true of the One becomes true of the other, as far as our position before God is concerned.

WHY DON'T I LIVE LIKE WHO I AM?

If you're an honest believer you're probably saying to yourself about now, "Well, God may say I'm holy and blameless, and victorious over sin and Satan because of my union with Christ, but it doesn't come out that way in my daily experience. There's something wrong somewhere!"

More than likely there *is* something wrong, and it probably has to do with your failure to understand the difference between your new eternal *position* in Christ and your daily *experience* of living the Christian life. One is what you are in God's estimation and the other is what you are in practice.

A clear distinction must be made between these two relationships which each believer has with Christ. Our new position or union with Christ is a *legal* status which we have with God, and it becomes absolutely true of us the instant we place saving faith in Christ — and it never changes. But our day-to-day living of the Christian life here in this world is the *experiential* side of redemption — it does vary from moment to moment. It all depends on whether by faith we walk with the Spirit of God in control or let our flesh dominate us.

OUR NEW POSSESSIONS AND BLESSINGS

Believers are the richest people in town! They are spiritual billionaires, if they only realize it. Paul reveals that God, **"has blessed us with every spiritual blessing in the heavenly places *in Christ*"** (Ephesians 1:3).

Now that's something to get excited about — but,

unfortunately, many believers don't. They would rather have some "*physical* experience down here in *earthly* places." This attitude only indicates they have never grasped that our "treasures are being stored in heaven" because that's where we actually are in God's mind. What we have down here is only temporary. What we accumulate here, if we are fortunate, will only benefit us for some eighty years — then someone else gets it.

When we have been born again, we instantly become citizens of heaven and eternal beings. We become aliens here — we are only on loan from our heavenly family. God doesn't want us to cling to the world and get too comfortable.

Dr. Lewis Chafer, founder of Dallas Theological Seminary, went through the Bible and counted thirty-three different spiritual blessings that become legally true of us the moment we believe.[1] These new possessions and positions are instantaneously and simultaneously declared to be ours in total at that moment.

In previous chapters of this book we looked at some of those spiritual blessings; justification, forgiveness, freedom, regeneration, new nature, acceptance with God, Christ's righteousness, reconciliation, no more condemnation, peace with God, a standing in grace, and redemption. There are at least twenty-one more eternal possessions that were given to us in the one package of salvation, and the thrill of the Christian life is finding out what these are and beginning to enjoy them here and now, not by and by.

OUR TWO RELATIONSHIPS WITH CHRIST

I think the chart on the next page will help to give us a better perspective of the two relationships a believer has with Christ. We have both a *positional* and *experiential* rela-

CHARACTERISTICS:
1) not experienced emotionally
2) not given progressively
3) not given on the basis of human merit
4) given for time and eternity at the instant of salvation
5) only realized by divine relation
6) they are brought about God alone with no help from man
7) this relationship is absolutely true of the believer, but is visible only to God

ETERNAL POSITION AND POSSESSIONS

reconcilliation

justification

new nature

forgiveness

YOU
IN
CHRIST

acccecptance
with God

freedom

righteousness

regeneration

new position

point of salvation ◄- - - - - - - - - - - - - - - - -

ETERNITY
TIME and SPACE

CHARACTERISTICS:
1) relates to the believer's walk while still on earth
2) the spokes represent what will be true in the life of the believer as he depends on the Holy Spirit.
3) this relationship affects our mind, emotion and body
4) these experiences grow as the believer matures in the Word and Faith.
5) unconfessed sin will hinder the expression of these Godly characteristics.
6) confessions and a renewed walk in the Spirit restores them.
7) this relationship is visible to both God and man.

"Keep walking in the Spirit and you will not fulfill the lusts of the flesh..."

fellowship
with believers

desire for Word

worship

fruit of the Spirit

YOU
IN
CHRIST

growth in faith

power in prayer

overcomes
temptation

power to
witness

GALATIANS 5:16

TEMPORAL (EARTHLY) EXPERIENCE

tionship. Our position in Christ is above time and space and is eternal. It is based entirely on the finished work of Christ on the cross. It is received *en toto* at the moment of salvation and cannot be diminished or improved upon by our behavior.

Our *temporal* relationship to Christ is only while we are in this life in time and space. The bottom circle on the chart illustrates that it is a matter of fellowship with Him. We can get out of fellowship with Christ by unbelief and known sin, but we can never get out of our position in Him because it is secured by the merit of Christ Himself.

In case it is not perfectly clear to you yet, the Bible teaches that once you've been born again you can *never* lose your salvation, because this eternal position will never cease to be true of you.

Your temporal experience changes from day to day as sin comes into your life, but your eternal position is a forever fact. How you behave in your daily walk with Christ can never change, in the slightest degree, your eternal relationship with Christ.

When you are born into your earthly family, you may be a winner or a loser in your behavior, but you're still a member of your family. There is no way to be unborn just because you don't measure up to the standards of your family. Your earthly parents might disown you, But God will never do that. You will be disciplined in grace for wrong behavior, but you won't be disowned.

Look at the chart carefully. The cross represents that moment when you believe in Christ's death on your behalf and are born again. At that instant the Holy Spirit puts you into a mystical, yet actual, intimate, physical union of life with Christ. You are at once made a member of His body, of His flesh and of His bone (Ephesians 5:30 NKJV).

As mentioned above, this relationship with Christ has two aspects, the eternal, invisible one in the heavenlies (where Christ sits) and the temporal (earthly) one while you're still alive here on earth.

God's act of placing you into Christ is called the "baptism of the Spirit" in 1 Corinthians 12:13: **"For by one Spirit we were all baptized into one body, whether Jews or Greeks, whether slaves or free, and we were all made to drink of one Spirit."** Paul likens union to the oneness a man and woman enter in marriage. In God's eyes it's a fact even though it usually takes a lot of tears and prayers to bring about an actual oneness in experience.

DYNAMICS OF TEMPORAL FELLOWSHIP

The Holy Spirit not only baptizes us into our eternal identification with Christ, He also at the same instant takes up permanent residence in our revived human spirits, and we come alive spiritually. He dwells in us in order to equip, motivate and empower us to live for Christ in this life.

In the lower circle of the chart I've shown just a few of the new characteristics that can be expected in the life of a believer who submits to the empowering of Christ through the Holy Spirit. When we yield to temptation and sin, Christ doesn't leave us, but the flesh or old self replaces Christ as the controlling influence in the life. If we stay in this condition for any length of time without judging it as sin and turning from it, we become carnal believers. But confessing our sin and once again authorizing Christ to take control restores our fellowship with Him.

With these things in mind, take time now to examine the chart. Notice particularly the eternal, permanent nature of our position in Christ. You'll see also that while we're still here on earth, Christ is to be the center of our lives, but it's the Holy Spirit who puts Him there as we walk in total dependence on Him to do so.

HOW DO I MAKE MY "POSITION" MY "EXPERIENCE"?

When God planned man's reconciliation, He obviously didn't mean for us to be holy and victorious in our "position" and weak and defeated in our "experience." His plan has always been that our position and experience be progressively brought into line with each other. But this only happens when we discover how fantastic our heavenly Father is and what He's made us to be *in Christ*.

A story I heard from Mark Twain's *The Prince and the Pauper* beautifully illustrates this point.

One day the King and Queen of a far-off country were bringing their new little Prince home from the royal hospital when their carriage collided with a poor pauper's cart. In this humble vehicle the poor man was bringing his wife and new baby home from the midwife's house. In the confusion, the two couples mistakenly picked up the wrong babies. So the little Prince went home to be raised by the pauper and his wife.

As this baby grew into childhood, he was forced to go into the streets and beg for food. He did not know that the very streets in which he begged were the property of his true father.

Day after day he would go to the palace and look through the iron fence at the little boy playing there and he would say to himself, "Oh, if only *I* were a Prince."

All his life he lived in poverty and want for one reason — he didn't know who he really was because he didn't
know who his father was.

BELIEVERS LIVE LIKE SPIRITUAL PAUPERS

But do you know that most true believers are doing
the same thing? They have never been taught *who* their real
Father is — the King of Kings and Lord of Lords. They don't
realize they're royal heirs to a royal throne. They are living in
self-imposed spiritual poverty, cheating themselves of the
experience of the riches of God's grace. I say the "experience" of them, because the riches are theirs whether they
enjoy them or not.

I read not long ago about a man who lived like a bum
for many years. He had been left a huge sum of money, but
the authorities couldn't locate him. They traced him from
flophouse to flophouse and finally found him asleep on a
fifty-cents-a-night cot in a mission. He was then informed of
His inheritance. He'd been rich for years but never knew it.
He had lived as a tramp needlessly.

When I heard about this I thought, "What a waste of
all those years." And that's just how I feel when I think of all
the wasted years of happiness and spiritual service that go
down the drain because "believers" are "unbelievers" when it
comes to taking God at His word when He tells us *who* we are
because of *whose* we are.

When we fail to live in the reality of our new position, daily experiencing the forgiveness, freedom, acceptance,
and empowering of the Spirit *(just to name a few of our spiritual riches)*, we short-change ourselves and the Lord. We
also rob the people whose lives we touch because they need
to see the reality of God in us.

OUR "POSITION" IS THE BASIS OF ALL VICTORY

I said at the beginning of this chapter that knowing and counting on our new position in Christ is the basis of all victorious and consistent Christian living. Why do I say that?

Because there's no other way to be set free from the *power* of the Law, the sin nature, and Satan. In Romans 1-5, Paul lays out the *redemptive* work of Christ and shows us that it's our remedy for the *penalty* of sins. But in chapters 6-8 of Romans Paul writes about our complete identification with Christ in His death, burial, and resurrection and shows that this is the remedy for overcoming the *power* of sin.

Unless God had dealt with the *power* of sin, we would be helpless victims of Satan's wiles and our own sin natures even though we are born again. There would be no hope of deliverance from depression, defeat, discouragement, failure, and doubt.

But praise God, His plan for our *complete* salvation includes a means of victory over sin's power, and it is based on our co-crucifixion and co-resurrection with Jesus Christ.

THE "OLD MAN" IS DEAD: R.I.P.!

In the chapter on Freedom, I gave an amplified version of the allegory Paul uses in Romans 7:14. Remember the woman who was married to a perfectionist tyrant and who could never satisfy his demands for perfection? Therefore she lived under constant condemnation. She finally met someone who was everything her husband was in the way of being perfect. But he was also filled with love and concern for her. She wanted to be joined to him, but the law said she would be an adulteress if she left her husband. She could be rid of her domineering mate if he would die, but he was in perfect health. The only other solution was for *her* to die, thereby effecting a legal separation from her husband. Then she would be free to marry anyone she chose. So she allowed her new lover to put her to death and then raise her back to life again. She was joined in marriage to him.

This allegory clearly applies to the truths taught in Romans 6, 7, and 8. If you understand this allegory, it will give you a good illustration of your union with Christ in His death, burial, and resurrection. You will see how the cross has set you free.

The tyrannical husband represents the Law, but by application includes the sin nature and Satan. The woman is the believer. The "other man" is Jesus.

The Law, sin, and Satan will never die as a threat while we are in this life. So God's solution was to crucify us with Jesus, thus legally breaking our relationship to these tyrants. Now we have been raised into a new life — the same resurrection life that Jesus now lives, a total victory over these enemies of our soul is possible.

On the basis of this legal severance of relationship, the authority of the old sin nature, the Law, and Satan have been broken. They do not have the legal right to touch us unless we allow it.

OUT OF ADAM, INTO CHRIST

Our union with Christ has also taken us legally out of our relationship to the first Adam and placed us into the Last Adam. We have become a partaker of all that He is. Both Adam and Christ demonstrate the principle that many can be affected for good or evil by the deed of one person.

In Romans 5:12-21 Paul shows this analogy between

Adam and Christ — the terrible condition Adam got mankind into and how Christ got us out. He says sin entered the race through Adam, but we were forgiven our sins through Christ. Death came by Adam's transgression, but life came to us by Christ's obedience. Our relationship to the first Adam made us dead *in* sin, but our crucifixion with Christ made us dead *to* sin. Our identification with Christ completely removes the effect of our identification with Adam.

The baptism of the Holy Spirit took us out of Adam and puts us into union with Christ. In fact, the word *baptism* means to totally identify one thing with another. It's the Greek word *baptizo*, and it was never translated into English from the original Greek; it was transliterated (which means to take the phonetics of a foreign word and make it a word in English). If we were to translate the word *baptizo* into its English equivalent, it would be the word "identification." So every time you read the word *baptized* in the Bible, you can mentally substitute the words *identified with.* This will give you a better understanding of the true meaning of this word which is so often misunderstood.

HE DIED FOR WHAT I "AM" AND WHAT I'VE "DONE"

We learned in the early chapters of this book that Christ bore our sins while He hung on the cross. In doing that He judged our sinful *deeds* and removed them as a barrier to God. But now we see not only were our *sins* put on Christ, but because of our identifion with Him, *we ourselves* were hanging there on the cross with Jesus.

By taking *us* to the cross with Him and then into the grave, He put to death not only our sinful *deeds,* but our sinful *selves.* This paid not only for what I *do,* but for what I *am.* This removes as a barrier not only what we did, but what we *are* — hostile to God, unrighteous, etc. This was even more important than atoning for our acts of sin, because we do what we do because of our sinful selves. He has provided *forgiveness* for what we've *done* and *deliverance* from what we *are.*

Now, not only are my sins no longer offensive to God, but I am not either. I am so accepted by the Father, because of my union with Christ, that He sees me as actually being seated in heaven in Christ. Paul emphasized this when he wrote, **"But God, being rich in mercy, because of His great love with which He loved us, even when we were dead in our transgressions, made us alive together with Christ...and raised us up with Him, and seated us with Him in the heavenly places in Christ Jesus"** (Ephesians 2:4-6).

IDENTIFIED WITH CHRIST
FROM THE CROSS TO THE THRONE

The key that unlocks the hidden truth of our release from Satan and the sin nature's power is the little preposition "in." We died *in* Christ, were buried *in* Him, resurrected *in* Him, are seated *in* Him, and will eventually reign *with* Him (Romans 6:1-13; Colossians 3:1-3; Revelation 20:6). Our entire ground for victory as a believer is wrapped up in the death-dealing blow that the death, burial, resurrection, and ascension of Jesus gave to the authority and power of Satan and sin. If you understood no other truths in the Bible than these and fully grasped your total identification with Christ in this victory, you'd be equipped to live victoriously over Satan and over the constant lure and pull of the flesh.

NO NEED TO BE CRUCIFIED DAILY:
ONCE WAS ENOUGH!

In one beautiful, all-inclusive statement in Galatians 2:20 Paul sums up the finality and the purpose of our crucifixion with Christ: **"I *have been* crucified with Christ; and it is no longer I who live, but Christ lives in me; and the life which I now live in the flesh I live by faith in the Son of God, who loved me, and delivered Himself up for me."**

Notice that Paul is careful to point out that our crucifixion with Christ is already a fact, not something which I must do to myself daily or try to get Christ to do to me at some point in my Christian life. In Romans 6, each time Paul speaks of our identification with Christ in His death, he uses the past tense of the verb: **"we *have been* buried with Him"** (verse 4); **"we *have become* united with Him in the likeness of His death"** (verse 5); **"our old self *was crucified* with Him"** (verse 6); **"we *have died* with Christ"** (verse 8).

Then Paul, on the basis of our *having been* crucified with Christ, makes the following powerful statement out of Romans 6:9-11:

—we are actually as dead to the sin nature's power as Jesus

—His victory over sin is also ours.

It goes without saying, if we have not yet claimed by faith our identification with Christ in His death and resurrection, we won't see Christ's victory as ours. Consequently we will not reckon ourselves dead to sin's power in our daily lives. We may valiantly struggle against temptation out of a genuine desire not to sin, but without reckoning upon our legitimate grounds for immunity to its power, our defenses will eventually wear down and we will give in to the sin nature.

WE DIED IN ORDER TO LIVE!

Knowing that we have been made dead to sin is only half the necessary information that leads to daily victorious Christian living. The other half of the co-crucifixion fact is that we have been made alive with Christ in order to experience His new resurrection kind of life. He is now totally free from the authority of Satan, sin, self, the flesh, and the Law of God. Paul urges believers to **"consider yourselves to be dead to sin, but alive to God in Christ Jesus"** (Romans 6:11).

Paul's statement in Galatians 2:20, that "he had been "crucified with Christ" yet was still alive, looks like a contradiction — unless we understand the truth of our union with Christ. How can you be both dead and alive at the same time? The answer to that is found in that same verse: **"It is no longer I who live, but Christ lives in me; and the life which I now live in the flesh I live by faith in the Son of God."** We're judicially declared dead to sin's power, but it only becomes a reality in our lives as we consider it to be fact and by faith count on Christ to live His life in and through us.

WHY ARE THESE "CO-CRUCIFIXION" TRUTHS HARD TO GRASP!

I'm under no illusions that everyone who has read the words in this last vital chapter has understood the depth of them. For 2,000 years these liberating truths have been prominent in Paul's teachings, particularly in Romans 6, 7, 8; Galatians and Colossians. Yet few believers have grasped their reality in daily coping with temptations of the flesh.

Why is this so?

I believe there are several reasons. First, as much as some believers would like it, there are no shortcuts to spiritual maturity just as there are no shortcuts to emotional and physical maturity. Both time and experiences of trials and error go into preparing us for an acceptance of these deeper life truths. If we have the notion that there is anything we can do in our own strength to improve our status with God and to resist the power of sin, then we'll miss God's solution.

I cannot begin to remember how many believers I have known, including myself, who have failed to claim our co-crucifixion with Christ and set out on rigorous programs of Bible study, prayer, scripture memorization, witnessing—and other "good religious activities" — in an effort to overcome sin and Satan's power.

The results all turn out about the same. At first, these activities seemed to help. But gradually what was started with enthusiasm ends up in a cycle of failure, self-recrimination and dedication of the flesh to try harder. This is where far too many believers spend most of their Christian lives.

If you have come to the point where you have no more formulas left for living victoriously, then there's one of three things you can do: (1) accept your defeat and live openly in the flesh with no pretense of trying to be godly or spiritual; (2) conclude that there isn't any real victory available but try to keep up a spiritual front so as not to be a bad testimony to others; or (3) thank God that He's finally revealed the path to victorious Christian living to you and stand by faith on your co-crucifixion with Christ to sin's power. Then reckon this eternal truth daily to be a fact in your life. Only then can the resurrected life of Christ — the Spirit-filled life — be consistently manifest through you. And only then can you say No to temptation and yield your new self to God.

When we take our stand on what God says about this, then we can fully expect to be delivered from sin's power. God promises, **"For sin shall not be master over you, for you are not under law, but under *grace*"** (Romans 6:14). Law demands and gives no help. Grace gives us the desire for God's will, then gives us the certainty of victory because our foe is defeated, and then provides the power to carry through.

BELIEVERS NEED TO BE "SON" CONSCIOUS

Another reason why believers fail to grasp the reality of their emancipation from sin's power is because so much preaching and teaching today is centered around our sinfulness and not around Christ's forgiveness. If we are "sin" conscious continually, then we cannot be "Son" conscious. Sin-consciousness only leads us to self-condemnation and self-effort to overcome the sin. But Son-consciousness continually reminds us of God's love and acceptance of us and the forgiveness which He purchased at the cross. *In short, we must focus on the problem Solver, not on the problem.*

Let's take a practical look at this concept. Nearly every believer has some area of his life where he feels God would like him to change. It may be a habit that isn't consistent with a Christian testimony or it may be an inner attitude of bitterness, jealousy, or lust. We spend much time in self-recrimination and anger at our inability to give up this sin. In fact, we're so absorbed in our problem that we have little time to focus on Jesus, the problem Solver. And because we are consumed with the consciousness of how sinful and unfaithful we are, we fail to appreciate the forgiveness and faithfulness of God. Our sin-consciousness will always lead us to some kind of *human* effort to change our behavior, and that path is always doomed to failure.

What is the solution to applying the work of the cross to our daily lives? How can we be consistently reminded to reckon ourselves dead to sin and alive to God?

ONLY A RENEWED MIND CAN GRASP THESE CO-CRUCIFIXION TRUTHS

When we are born into the family of God, we bring with us the accumulation of attitudes, behavior patterns, complexes, addictions and experiences from our spiritually dead life. All these have combined to make us the person we are. Now suddenly the Bible tells you that you are a "new creation" in Christ. "The old has passed away, behold, the new has come." God also says He now sees us as "holy and blameless" in His sight because we are "hidden in Christ" and clothed with His righteousness (2 Corinthians 5:17,21; Colossians 1:22; 3:3).

The question now is, how do we make what God says is true of us more real in our minds than what we see in our performance? Most of us know we have been anything but holy and blameless. For some, there are probably a number of things you have not been able to forgive yourself for, let alone accept God's forgiveness for them.

The Bible gives us one basic answer. We must have our minds flushed of the lingering consciousness of the old self-life and a whole new viewpoint of ourselves put in its place. We must have our minds renewed before our behavior can consistantly change.

How does this take place?

Paul says in Romans 12:2 that the only way to be transformed and not conform to the old way you used to behave is to have your mind renewed. Then the Psalmist tells us how this is done: **"How can a young man** [and woman] **keep his way pure? By keeping it according to Thy word...Thy word I have treasured in my heart, that I may not sin against Thee"** (Psalm 119:9,11).

There's no way to have our minds renewed apart from the cleansing and nurturing power of God's Word. The writer of Hebrews calls the Word "milk" and "meat" because it's that which gives us growth and understanding (Hebrews 5:12-14). Countless believers are struggling along trying to keep their heads above water spiritually. In almost every case I have counseled, they had no regular intake of the Word, Christian literature or tapes. There's just no way to find out about the incredible new person you've been made to be apart from its revelation in God's Word. You won't be consistently reminded to reckon yourself dead to the flesh and Satan's ploys unless you regularly take in God's viewpoint.

YOUR "NEW SELF" MEANS THAT YOU CAN HAVE A NEW SELF-IMAGE

The world, the flesh, and the Devil don't let up on us just because we have been born again. In fact, that's when the real conflict begins. The Devil will really work to keep you conscious of all your faults and failures. He doesn't want to see the brand new creation God has made us. He knows that if he can keep with a sense of inferiority before God, we won't be a threat to his kingdom.

The science of psycho-cybernetics — which is a study of the effect of self-image on behavior — has clinically demonstrated that you cannot act consistently contrary to your self-image — that which you conceive yourself to be.

We have all developed a complete image of ourselves, especially in our first sixteen years. Unless there is some kind of radical intervention that changes our self image, we will persistently act in a way consistent with what we believe about ourselves.

Dr. Maxwell Maltz, a plastic surgeon who had years of experience observing people's preoperative and postoperative self-images, said in his book *Psycho-cybernetics* that even after surgery had successfully removed ugly disfigurements, some people still behaved as though they looked the same. They just could not let go of their old self-image. Their self-image was so deeply ingrained that it was virtually impossible to accept their new appearance, even with the evidence starring back at them from a mirror.

Yet Dr. Maltz observed a definite phenomenon in other patients. Within several weeks after the plastic surgery had removed an ugly scar, corrected a large nose, or some unattractive feature, some patients began to experience a change in their whole personality and behavior. Those who had previously let their disfigurement give them an inferiority complex began to be very self-confident and outgoing. Others who had been failures in one thing or another began to see themselves as winners, and when they did, they actually became more successful in their endeavors.

After twenty years of observing this, Dr. Maltz rightly concluded that it's impossible to behave consistently different from the way you see yourself.

But as startling as this discovery was to the field of science, it is a principle as old as the Bible. This is the heart of what it means to be a "new creation" in Christ. When I believe and accept who God says I am in Christ, then I'll begin to behave like it. As I let the Holy Spirit renew my

mind through God's Word to really understand and believe all
the things God has once and for all given me in Christ, then
will I begin to be transformed into His image and likeness.

My *self* image can be changed only when I count true
that I've got a whole new self inside of me that God created
in His likeness (Ephesians 4:23-24). That new self is beautiful to God because He created it. I don't need to be afraid of
what men or God see in me, because God created the new self
and forgave me for the old.

A CLOSING WORD OF PERSONAL TESTIMONY

I began this book with my personal story. I sought to
share what a miracle it was that God pursued me and brought
me into His forever family. One of the chief purposes for
writing this book was to show how great God's Father-heart
is in the way He provided reconciliation for all mankind.

But I have also wanted to show Christ not only as our
reconciler, but as the healer of broken hearts and damaged
lives. No one could have been more fouled up in his personal
life than I was. My self-image was so bad I sometimes con-
templated suicide. I felt the world would be better off without someone like me. Even after I became a true believer in
Christ I have often been inhibited for God's use because of
feelings of unworthiness.

It wasn't until I learned about my new eternal position in Christ and the thirty-three new possessions He had
conferred upon me that I began to feel like a different person.
No one else had ever thought so highly of me. As I continued
to find out more about this great God who had loved me so
much that He put me into union with His Son, I had a greater
appreciation of *who* I was because of *whose* I was. My Father

is a King, so that makes me a member of the royal family.

As you read this book, my sincere hope is that you will see Jesus and yourself in a whole new light. If you've needed to be reconciled to God, I pray that you have been. If you've needed to be liberated from a quagmire of self-life and defeat, I trust you've seen the provision God has made for your liberation.

But most of all, I pray that you have come to see more of God's amazing grace — which was made available to you through the cross.

You were made to soar with "God's eagles." In Christ you're lifted above the damage and fetters of sin on the "wings of eagles" (Isaiah 40:28-31). Settle back in faith and begin to enjoy this "so great salvation" that has been all provided by God's AMAZING GRACE.

I'll see you in the heavenlies,

Hal Lindsey, saved by grace.

When we've been there ten thousand years,
bright shining as the sun;
We've no less days to sing God's praise,
than when we first begun.

—Captain John Newton

Hal Lindsey's
International Intelligence Briefing

This Monthly Inside Report Uncovers and Explores Worldwide Events

If you'd like to discover how worldwide events are pointing to the last days . . .

. . . then you should be reading *Hal Lindsey's International Intelligence Briefing* — the amazing newsletter that gives you an insider's view and perspective on world events.

The Significance of World Events

Every day our worldwide intelligence network scours the world for little-known, but significant news events. The information is then studied and analyzed by Hal Lindsey and his staff to uncover its Biblical significance.

Then every month we put together a concise, insightful report that reveals how these events fit together and what they could mean for your future.

Many of them are in the news every day. For example, you'll get up-to-date reports on . . .

- What's happening in the Middle East? Is peace around the corner? Or war?
- The true state of our military. Are we prepared for the next conflict?
- What's next for the economy.
- Military hot spots and world conflicts.

News Events That Impact Your Future

But it's not just everyday news. We delve deeper and interpret lesser-known news events for you.

- Killer viruses are back. Are they part of the great plagues prophesied for the Last Days?

Matching the News With Biblical Scenarios

Hal Lindsey relates these events to Biblical prophecy, and shows how many of them fit the scenarios laid out in Ezekial 38-39 and Matthew 24.

You'll learn which events are setting the stage for the final battles as described in the book of Revelation.

With Hal Lindsey's *International Intelligence Briefing* you'll know what's happening right now and what to expect in the future. It's your indispensable source for the news of the world from a Biblical perspective.

A one-year (12-issue) subscription to *International Intelligence Briefing* is just $40. And you're fully protected by our . . .

Money-Back Guarantee

Read your first three issues of *International Intelligence Briefing*. If you aren't completely satisfied then let us know within 90 days and we'll send you a full refund of every penny you paid.

To subscribe just pick up the phone and call TOLL-FREE:

1-800-848-8735

Or write your name and address on a piece of paper and mail it with your check of $40 to HLM, P.O. Box 4000, Palos Verdes, CA 90274.

With Hal Lindsey's *International Intelligence Briefing* you'll know what to expect in the months and years ahead. Subscribe today. And don't forget the money-back guarantee. Thank you.